THE FOURTEENTH AMENDMENT AND THE STATES

Da Capo Press Reprints in

AMERICAN CONSTITUTIONAL AND LEGAL HISTORY

GENERAL EDITOR: LEONARD W. LEVY

Claremont Graduate School

THE FOURTEENTH AMENDMENT AND THE STATES

A Study of the Operation of the Restraint Clauses
of Section One of the Fourteenth Amendment
to the Constitution of the United States

by
Charles Wallace Collins

SPRINGER SCIENCE+BUSINESS MEDIA, LLC 1974

Library of Congress Cataloging in Publication Data

Collins, Charles Wallace, 1879-1964.
The Fourteenth amendment and the states.

(Da Capo Press reprints in American constitutional and legal history)
Reprint of the ed. published by Little, Brown, Boston.
1. United States. Constitution. 14th amendment.
2. State rights. I. Title.
KF4558.14th.C64 1974 342'.73'04 74-5437
ISBN 978-1-4757-1444-9 ISBN 978-1-4757-1442-5 (eBook)
DOI 10.1007/978-1-4757-1442-5

This Da Capo Press edition of *The Fourteenth Amendment and the States* is an unabridged republication of the first edition published in Boston in 1912.

Published by Da Capo Press, Inc.

Springer Science+Business Media New York 1974
Originally published by Plenum Publishing Corporation New York in 1974

THE FOURTEENTH AMENDMENT AND THE STATES

THE FOURTEENTH AMENDMENT AND THE STATES

A STUDY OF THE OPERATION OF THE RESTRAINT CLAUSES OF SECTION ONE OF THE FOURTEENTH AMENDMENT TO THE CONSTITUTION OF THE UNITED STATES

BY

CHARLES WALLACE COLLINS, M.A.

SOMETIME FELLOW IN THE UNIVERSITY OF CHICAGO

MEMBER OF THE ALABAMA BAR

BOSTON

LITTLE, BROWN, AND COMPANY

1912

Printers
S. J. PARKHILL & CO., BOSTON, U.S.A.

TO

MY FATHER AND MY MOTHER

PREFACE

THE studies here presented are the outgrowth of a paper read before the Government Club of Harvard University in February, 1911. Some of them have within recent months appeared, in substantially their present form, in certain of the academic and legal journals.

In the preparation of the statistical material the author has made no use of the current digests of decisions, annotations to the Constitution, nor of the indices to the Supreme Court Reports, except by way of comparison of results. He has gone directly to the body of the Reports and given each case a personal examination.

Much repetition will be found throughout the work. This may detract from its logical unity, but it is hoped that it may serve some purpose. The true nature of the Fourteenth Amendment to the Constitution of the United States is little known. The processes of its operation are intricate and complex. This reiteration, therefore, of certain salient features may not be amiss in serving to render more familiar a subject that, although not new historically, has been scantily discussed.

The author's thanks are due to the editors of the following periodicals for the courtesy of extending to him the copyright privileges for the use of the material in the chapters mentioned below: The *American Law Review* for Chapters V and VI; the *Yale Law Journal* for Chapter VII; the *Columbia Law Review* for Chapter VIII; and the *South Atlantic Quarterly* for Chapter X. The author desires also to express his appreciation of the privileges extended to him while in the Library of Congress.

CHARLES WALLACE COLLINS.

WASHINGTON, May, 1912.

TABLE OF CONTENTS

TABLE OF CHARTS

TABLE OF CASES CITED

TABLE OF LAWS CITED

State laws declared unconstitutional in whole or in part by the Supreme Court of the United States, under the operation of the Fourteenth Amendment, appear in small capitals.

THE FOURTEENTH AMENDMENT AND THE STATES

CHAPTER I

INTRODUCTION [1]

AT the close of the Civil War the Republican Party found itself in full control of every branch of the Federal Government. That Party had become in a large degree the repository of the national spirit. It was preëminently the Union party, and to it was entrusted the sovereign power. The country had passed through a great crisis. The political theories of the South had been put to the test of the sword and were now discredited. Slavery was gone and the Southern States were subordinated to Federal authority. The

[1] Outside of the source material as evidenced by the governmental records and other contemporary writings, the following works have been consulted with profit in the preparation of this chapter: Rhodes, *History of the United States*, Vols. V, VI, and VII; Dunning, *Reconstruction — Political and Economic;* Burgess, *Reconstruction and the Constitution;* Haynes, *Life of Sumner;* McCall, *Life of Stevens;* Blaine, *Twenty Years of Congress;* McPherson, *History of Reconstruction;* Fleming, *Civil War and Reconstruction in Alabama;* Fleming, *Documentary History of Reconstruction;* and Flack, *The Adoption of the Fourteenth Amendment.*

Republican Party set itself to the stupendous and unparalleled task of reconstructing the Union along the lines of the political theories which had been vindicated by the outcome of the War.

It was not a time when men could act in the coolness of deliberation. Hardly had the boom of the cannon ceased or the groans of the dying been hushed before many problems pressed for immediate consideration and action. At an early stage certain of these questions began to assume definite shape. The negroes, nearly five million in number, must be looked after. Their status needed to be defined and fixed. The territory formerly occupied by the seceding States must be reorganized and under certain conditions readmitted into the Union. The rule of the Republican Party must be established and perpetuated. This latter was considered of prime importance even by broadminded Union men of non-partisan tendencies. It was felt that the Democratic Party could not be entrusted with any part of the solution of the problem of reconstruction. To the mind of the North a Democratic victory would have meant the triumph of the forces of the Rebellion. This sentiment was normal in 1865. In the later campaigns it became increasingly abnormal. The continual waving of the "bloody shirt" throughout the political campaigns of the next ten years caused a reaction in the North which finally restored the normal issues of the day.

Since the life of the Republic had undergone an extraordinary change within the decade preceding 1865, it was felt necessary that the organic law of the land should give voice to the new principles that had been thus evolved. The Constitution of the United States required certain amendments that it might express and preserve the results of the struggle which culminated in the overthrow of the Confederacy. On January 31, 1865 the proposed Thirteenth Amendment abolishing slavery passed the House by the necessary two-thirds majority. Since slavery had already been practically abolished, the measure attracted no great attention.

A proposed Fourteenth Amendment was introduced in the House by Thaddeus Stevens on December 5, 1865. Other proposals followed in quick succession. Already on March 3, 1865, the Freedman's Bureau had been created. Before discussion of the Fourteenth Amendment had assumed definite shape a civil rights act was adopted, April 9, 1866. This purported to elevate the freedmen to the plane of political and social equality with the white people. The constitutionality of this act was seriously questioned, even by members of the Republican Party. The fight on the adoption of the Fourteenth Amendment was long and hard.[1] From the time of its proposal in Congress

[1] In this study we are concerned primarily with section one of the Amendment. Although as finally adopted it contained five sections, it was the first section that was

to its final proclamation was a period of nearly three years of constant and bitter struggle. The resolution as originally introduced was a much stronger centralizing measure than the Amendment as finally adopted. It practically threw all legislative power into the hands of the Federal Government, leaving the State governments to operate only according to the will of Congress. This met with serious opposition from the conservative wing of the Republican Party and necessitated a long series of debates, committals, recommittals, and compromises.

The resolution, in practically its final form, passed the House on May 10, 1866, passed the Senate with the amendment adding the citizenship clause on June 8, 1866, and was concurred in by the House on June 13, 1866. Sections two, three, and four related to the Southern problem. They were temporary measures growing out of a highly abnormal situation. They gave voice to no permanent constitutional principle, but their incorporation into the Amendment made section one easier of passage and made the whole measure an appeal to the passions and prejudices of the masses at the North.

The proposed Amendment was submitted to the States for ratification on June 16, 1866. This was followed by the prompt rejection of the measure by all

possessed of great vitality and marked a new departure in the American political ideal. The other sections may have been better adapted to stump speeches and campaign thunder, but section one alone was of permanent importance.

of the Southern States. Later historians have criticised the South for this action. It is said that had the South accepted the conditions imposed by the Amendment without murmur, she would have been spared the awful tragedy of the Reconstruction. But the South was asked to choose, and she chose according to her own ideals. A people of spirit could not have done otherwise. The Amendment not only ran counter to her conceptions of constitutional government, but also required her to voluntarily disfranchise those who had led her in a cause which she believed to be just.

By the spring of 1868, nearly two years after the submission of the measure to the States, more than three-fourths of all of the Northern States had voted for ratification. Ohio, New Jersey, and Oregon had ratified the Amendment in 1866; the Democrats were victorious at the polls in the next election, following which, in 1868, each of these States passed resolutions rescinding their former ratifications. This action was repudiated by Congress. The border States of Maryland, Delaware, and Kentucky rejected the Amendment outright. California, having a deadlock in the Legislature over the measure, took no action in the matter. There still remained the South. Were the Southern States still members of the Union, or were they territories subject to the control of Congress? Opinions in Congress differed widely. Some of the Radicals thought that the Amendment needed no further ratification, since the North was the Union. On the other hand, the Conservatives held that the South was never out of the Union, and hence the votes of the Southern States must be counted in arriving at the three-fourths majority necessary for ratification. There was much confusion on this point, and final action was based upon a compromise which was logically absurd. The Southern States were both outside and inside of the Union at the same time. They were outside because they were excluded from all representation in Congress and because certain conditions imposed by Congress must be met before they could reënter. One of these conditions was that they assist the Northern States in adopting a Fourteenth Amendment to the Constitution of the United States! Otherwise they must remain outside of the Union.

They were inside of the Union because the Amendment could not become a part of the Constitution without their favorable action. On the basis of this theory it was submitted to them in 1866, and their vote counted in 1868 in the final result. There were two logical positions that might have been taken by Congress: First, to consider the Southern States as within the Union, allowing them the privileges thereto appertaining; and second, to consider them as territories outside of the Union and to proclaim the Amendment adopted when the necessary three-fourths of the Northern States had ratified it. This latter course would have had the desired effect of making the Amendment a condition precedent to all territories entering the Union.

Under the Congressional plan of reconstruction the South, in 1868, found itself under the domination of what is generally called the "carpet-bag-scalawag-negro" rule. This new régime thus set up in the South by Federal authority ratified the Fourteenth Amendment in 1868 with an avidity and unanimity of which no other section of the country could boast, not even New England. Following this action the Secretary of State proclaimed the Fourteenth Amendment as a part of the Supreme Law of the Land, on July 28, 1868, having been ratified by the necessary three-fourths of the States of the Union.

What was the motive and the aim of the Republican Party in adopting the Fourteenth Amendment? These may be resolved into four elements, to wit: —

(1) The punishment of the South. Charles Sumner, a radical idealist, and Thaddeus Stevens, a radical partisan,[1] led the victorious radical wing of the Republi-

[1] Professor Dunning characterizes the two men as follows: As to Sumner, "he was a perfect type of that narrow fanaticism which erudition and egotism combine to produce, and to which political crises alone give opportunity for actual achievement." As to Stevens he writes, "Stevens, truculent, vindictive, and cynical, dominated the House of Representatives in the second session of this (the Thirty-ninth) Congress with even less opposition than in the first. A keen and relentlessly logical mind, an ever-ready gift of biting sarcasm and stinging repartee, and a total lack of scruple as to means in the pursuit of a legislative end, secured him an ascendency in the House which none of his party associates ever dreamed of disputing." — *Reconstruction — Political and Economic* by W. A. Dunning in *The American Nation*, Vol. XXII, pp. 86–87. Edited by A. B. Hart.

can Party in the Senate and in the House, respectively. Those who had seceded from the Union were regarded as rebels and traitors. It was thought expedient and necessary that some penalty should be enforced against them and that certain precautionary measures should be taken to insure the safety of the future. This sentiment found voice in sections two, three, and four of the Amendment. Section two was intended to enforce negro suffrage by preventing the Southern States from disfranchising them upon pain of reduced representation in Congress. Section three disfranchised from State and Federal office, civil and military, practically all of the white people of the South, leaving the affairs of government in the hands of "carpet-baggers," "scalawags," and negroes. Section four made it impossible, should the South return to power in Congress, that the national debt should be questioned, or that pensions should be paid to Confederate soldiers, or that any debt incurred in aid of the Confederacy should be recognized by a State or by the United States.

These three sections were popular in conception, easily understood by the masses, and were seized upon by the Radicals as a political expedient. In effect they formed the party platform of 1866. In the campaign which followed, these sections were emphasized before the people. It was an appeal to fanaticism, fear, and revenge. The real vital element of the Amendment lay in section one. The revolutionary doctrines therein contained were couched in vague and general terms. When read by the average voter it meant little or nothing. On the basis of this section the party could make no effective appeal, consequently it was lost sight of in the fierce and bitter campaign of 1866, where the flames of passion were fanned by the constant waving of the "bloody shirt." This punitive element in the motive for the adoption of the Amendment was the largest factor in securing its ratification. Nobody understood section one. Everybody understood sections two, three, and four.

(2) The elevation of the negro to the plane of equality with the white race. This was to be accomplished through legislation by Congress under section five by way of enforcement of section one. One of the fundamental reasons for the adoption of section one was that it would give constitutional validity to the Civil Rights Act of 1866, which was passed for the benefit of the negro. The first section of the Amendment was generally supposed to have no other effect than to uplift and protect the freedmen. In so far as the masses comprehended the measure, this was their interpretation. Many men of thought and reflection shared the popular view. At this time the negro question bulked large in the public mind and formed, along with other Southern questions, the keynote of every political campaign.

(3) The centralization of large powers into the hands of the Federal Government — powers hitherto exercised by the States. This purpose is related to the foregoing.

In order for Congress to gain control over the negro situation in the South it was necessary that the power of the Federal Government be extended and increased. This would have the effect of withdrawing from the States much authority and power which they had exercised under the old Constitution. The Amendment was written in general terms, making use of constitutional phrases long known to all English-speaking peoples. The Republican Party expected to interpret these clauses so that they would become the concrete embodiment of a new national ideal. The States' Rights theory was in disrepute. In the final test of sovereignty — physical force — the national spirit had won. This feeling of national solidarity had long been growing in the North. It was greatly strengthened by the War. Now, in the flush of victory, it was expressing itself through its organization, the Republican Party. The radical wing of this party was willing to go to great lengths in making changes in the governmental system. They knew what they intended by the vague terms of section one of the Amendment. They knew that it could be interpreted so as to extend far out beyond the negro race question. They desired to nationalize all civil rights; to make the Federal power supreme; and to bring the private life of every citizen directly under the eye of Congress. This intention of the Radicals, though too much involved for the people in general to comprehend, was quite generally understood by the leading editors in the North and in the South and by the party leaders on both sides.

(4) To more firmly establish and maintain the control of the Government by the Republican Party. This party was the Union party. It claimed the credit of saving the nation. At the close of the War it was felt that the perpetuation of the Union depended upon the perpetuation of the Republican Party. The Democratic stronghold was still in the South. To readmit them to the political life of the nation on the basis of an increased representation on account of the abolition of slavery would imperil the supremacy of the party of the Union. This was altogether unthinkable. One of the immediate purposes of the adoption of the Amendment was to assist in destroying the power of the Democratic Party in the South and in its place to build up Republicans. This result was to be obtained by disfranchising the whites and enfranchising the blacks. Many of the Radicals thought that a fifteenth amendment to the Constitution was unnecessary in gaining this end.

This party purpose was made no secret. Democrats in general were regarded as disloyal and Southern Democrats as traitors. It was an axiom that the safety of the Union depended on sustaining the control of the Republican Party. Shortly after the adoption of the Amendment Mr. Blaine could say with pride: "It had been carried from first to last as a party measure — unanimously supported by the Republicans, unanimously opposed by the Democrats." It "failed to attract the vote of a single Democratic member in any State Legislature in the whole Union."[1]

The opposition of the Democratic Party to the adoption of the Fourteenth Amendment was something more than a fight for self-preservation. It was a struggle to maintain the time-honored principles upon which that party was founded. The Democratic Party had always stood for local government where only local interests were involved. It had worked on the theory that the Federal Government possessed and should possess only delegated powers — that its sphere of activity was circumscribed by definite limitations. Many of its leaders had been Union men. All of them, especially at the North, accepted the results of the War as being the defeat of the doctrine of secession. But they saw in section one of the Amendment the possibility of a fundamental change in our system of government. Couched in language pleasing to the ear, in phrases sacred to all men of English stock, there were given to the Federal Government powers of consolidation and centralization which would put the whole country into the hands of the party in power. For these reasons the Democratic Party strained every nerve to prevent its adoption. It was a hopeless fight and one destined to defeat, but it has left on record much that is instructive for future generations.

The South, being excluded from Congress, had no

[1] Blaine, *Twenty Years of Congress*, Vol. II, p. 309.

share in the fight there against the measure. The struggle was there carried on by Northern men alone. The general stand taken by the Democratic Party may be stated by quoting from a speech of Representative Chanler of New York, delivered on the floor of the House on January 23, 1866: "Centralization, sir, is the constant and direct tendency of all of these measures. The temper of the people just come from the stern and bloody conflict of a civil war is not calm and sedate. The people are scarcely free from the oppressive laws which a military despotism laid upon them mountain high. The innocent and the guilty, Union men and rebels alike, were held down by the military despotism which necessity forced upon the country; and now, when the hand of power is just loosed from the throats of the people, and before they are allowed time to breathe freely, you rush upon them and demand immediate and prompt action on questions which involve the greatest interests of every individual, not only in the South, but in the North, questions which have occupied the long and serious deliberation of the wisest and best men the country has ever produced. . . . Sir, the grand distinctive policy of this government is that all power arises from the people, and that all power that descends upon the people is exceptional and hostile to the spirit of our Constitution and to the whole system of our government in form and in spirit."[1]

[1] *Congressional Globe*, 1865–1866, Part I, p. 383.

Having lost the fight in Congress, the Democrats renewed the struggle with increased vigor before the State Legislatures when the proposed Amendment was submitted for ratification. For nearly three years the measure was before the States. During all of this time the Democratic press was a unit against it. North and South the pros and cons of these remarkable politico-military campaigns were flared before the people. The Republicans used the machinery of the Government and "waved the bloody shirt." The Democrats everywhere with one voice raised the cry of protest and warning. "Wherever the Democrats were in majority," says Mr. Blaine, "the Legislature rejected it, and in every Legislature where the Republicans had control the Democrats in minority voted against it."[1] Furthermore, as we have seen, the Democratic Legislatures of Ohio, New Jersey, and Oregon, upon coming into power in 1868 promptly passed resolutions rescinding the ratification of the Amendment by the previous Republican Legislatures in those States, while the Southern States when Democratic in 1866 rejected the Amendment immediately. Mr. Blaine remarks further: "It is very seldom in the history of political issues, even when partisan feeling is most deeply developed, that so absolute a division is formed as was recorded upon the question of adopting the Fourteenth Amendment." On this measure he says "the line of Democratic hostility in the Nation and

[1] Blaine, *Twenty Years of Congress*, pp. 309, 310.

in the State was absolutely unbroken."[1] To the Republicans this action of the Democrats was a stigma of disgrace. To the Democrats it was a badge of honor.

The grounds of Democratic opposition to the Amendment may be briefly summarized as follows: —

1. As a measure of the Republican Party one of its chief effects would be to decrease the Democratic Party by disfranchising from public office its Southern constituency.

2. The times were too abnormal for the proper consideration of a constitutional amendment.

3. The radical change in the system of government which might be effected under section one could lead to the practical abolition of the State governments.

4. It was an undemocratic measure in that the people to be most affected by its operation would have no voice in proposing it, and, under the political methods employed, no voice in its adoption.

Several years after the adoption of the Amendment, when the various clauses thereof came up to the Supreme Court of the United States for interpretation, the majority of the Court followed, in effect, the reasoning of the Democratic opposition, and refused to give effect to the ideals of the Radical Republicans.

Having secured the adoption of the Amendment, the Republican Party then set out to give it force and effect. The Congressional ideal of the purpose and of the enforcement of the Amendment at this time was

[1] Blaine, *Twenty Years of Congress*, pp. 309, 310.

simply an expression of the aims of the Radicals who were in full control. We can gather from the laws they enacted what they intended the Fourteenth Amendment to be. The first enforcement act was passed May 31, 1870.[1] This was supplemented by an amendatory act February 28, 1871.[2] These two acts may be considered together. They had three aims in view, to wit: To protect negro voters under the Fifteenth Amendment; to reënact the Civil Rights Act of 1866 under the Fourteenth Amendment, thereby rendering it constitutional; and, lastly, to place all violations of these acts under Federal control by giving to the Federal Courts exclusive jurisdiction of such alleged violations, and by giving to the President of the United States the power to use the Army and Navy to enforce its provisions. The penalties for violating these acts were exceedingly heavy. The minimum cost to the party offending would be more than one thousand dollars for each offence, a cash sum which was hard for anybody in the South to get together in those days.

The next enforcement act, commonly known as the Ku Klux Act, was passed April 20, 1871.[3] Its purpose was to enforce all of the provisions of section one of the Fourteenth Amendment. This law was a drastic measure. It was aimed primarily at the acts of private persons against private persons. Under its provi-

[1] Acts and Resolutions, 41 Cong. 2 Sess., p. 95.
[2] *Ibid.*, 3 Sess., p. 45.
[3] *Ibid.*, 41 Cong. 1st Sess., p. 294.

sions the accused party could not avail himself of the defence that he was acting under State laws. The law did not mention the negro race, but was universal in its application. It was a nationalization of all civil rights. The Federal Courts had universal jurisdiction. The States were powerless to regulate their own internal affairs.

Section one made any person civilly liable in damages who interfered with the rights of another as secured to him by the Fourteenth Amendment. Section two provided that any persons who should conspire to deprive any citizen of the United States of the equal protection of the laws should be liable to fine and imprisonment through the Federal Courts. The minimum penalty was a fine of five hundred dollars, while the maximum penalty was a fine of five thousand dollars and six years imprisonment in addition to civil liability as provided in section one. Section three gave the President of the United States the authority to employ the Army and Navy to quell domestic disturbances within a State. Section four authorized the President to suspend by proclamation the writ of *habeas corpus* in any portion of the Union when, in his opinion, there was organized and powerful resistance to State or Federal authority. Section five disqualified for jury service in the Federal Courts all persons who were involved in such rebellions against the government.

Section six of this statute represents the climax of the Congressional ideal of the scope of the Fourteenth Amendment. It provided, in substance, that if any person by reasonable diligence could have prevented or assisted in preventing any persons from depriving another person or persons of the equal protection of the laws and did not do so, that person should be liable in damages in a civil action in the Federal Courts in a sum not exceeding five thousand dollars. A more remarkable law was never written upon the statute books of an English-speaking people! How far had Congress strayed from the ideals of law and government set up by their forefathers in England and America! Here was a law compelling every person in the United States to see that his neighbor's rights were properly secured and enforced!

This law was aimed at the operations of the Ku Klux Klan in the South, but it rests on the same plane as the Fourteenth Amendment and applied equally to all persons in the Union. It was unlimited in its terms as to time, place, or persons, and had it not been declared unconstitutional by the Supreme Court it would have worked a revolution in the American Government.

The last enforcement measure of Congress was the Civil Rights Act of March 1, 1875.[1] For nearly five years it had been, in one form or another, before Congress. It was the darling measure of Charles Sumner, and he used all of the force of his powerful personality to secure its passage. Time and again he would bring it up in the Senate and plead for it with tears in his

[1] United States Statutes at Large, Vol. XVIII, p. 335.

eyes. These were his dying words to Hoar: "You must take care of the Civil Rights Bill — my bill — the Civil Rights Bill — don't let it fail!"[1] About two months after his death the Senate passed a civil rights bill, but it did not reach a vote in the House before adjournment.

In the elections of 1874 the Republicans lost control of the House of Representatives and had their majority in the Senate seriously reduced. The tide had turned. The short session ending with the spring of 1875 was the last lease of power to the Radicals in Congress. Under the leadership of Benjamin F. Butler they passed the Civil Rights Bill, which became a law March 1, 1875. This law had for its purpose the obliteration of the color line in the South, and to give to the negroes the full and equal privileges of all hotels, street cars, passenger trains, steamboats, or other public conveyances, by land or water; of theatres and all other places of public amusements. It was, however, a milder law than the one sought by Sumner in that it did not attempt to obliterate the color line in churches, schools, and cemeteries.

Any person who violated the provisions of this act was liable to a forfeiture of five hundred dollars to the party aggrieved and to a minimum fine in the Federal Courts of five hundred dollars in addition to the costs of each proceeding. While this law was intended for immediate application in the South, it applied equally

[1] Haynes, *Sumner*, p. 433. Sumner died March 11, 1874.

to every part of the Union. It is of interest to notice that when in 1883 five cases came up to the Supreme Court of the United States to test the constitutionality of the act, only one was from a Southern State.

We are thus enabled to see what was the Congressional interpretation of the Fourteenth Amendment. The same force in the Republican Party which secured the adoption of the Amendment has also given us its ideal of the purpose and scope of that constitutional measure by the laws thereunder enacted. They meant to change the form of the American Commonwealth. The States were to exist only in name. Their legislatures and their courts were to be reduced to impotency. The citizens of the States were now to live directly under the surveillance of the Federal Government, looking to it for protection in his private affairs and fearing its avenging power should he transgress the least of its commandments.

Into the hands of Congress was placed the sovereign power of the Nation. No longer was the National Government to be one of delegated powers, and no part of the sovereign power was to be held any longer by the States. Section one of the Fourteenth Amendment was intended ultimately to create out of the former Union one centralized consolidated government with the supreme power vested in the Federal authorities in Washington. Such was the ideal of the Radicals.

CHAPTER II

The Dilemma of the Supreme Court

Shortly after the adoption of the Fourteenth Amendment the Radicals lost control of the Republican Party and of Congress. Sumner and Stevens were dead. The flames of passion were slowly reducing themselves to ashes. Public opinion had declared against any violent change in the form of the Government, and the country was beginning to breathe the breath of normal health.

The burden of interpreting the Amendment and the laws enacted by Congress for its enforcement naturally befell the duty of the Supreme Court of the United States. Both the conservative and the radical wings of the Republican Party were represented in that tribunal. The first case involving the Amendment came up for final hearing five years after its adoption.[1] The Court was by no means unmindful of its vast importance. It was twice argued before the Court. Mr. Justice Miller in delivering the majority opinion made this significant statement: "We do not conceal from ourselves the great responsibility which this duty devolves upon

[1] The Slaughter House Cases, 16 Wall. 36. Decided April 14, 1873.

us. No questions so far-reaching and pervading in their consequences, so profoundly interesting to the people of this country, and so important in their bearings on the relations of the United States, have been before this Court during the official lifetime of any of its present members."[1] By a decision of five to four the Court repudiated the radical ideal of the scope of the "privileges or immunities" clause of the Amendment, taking the practical view that the police power of the States still remained in force.

Two years later another case reached the Court for decision, involving the power of Congress to pass laws by way of enforcing the Amendment.[2] It also involved an interpretation of the nature of the Amendment in its relation to wrongs done by individuals to individuals acting in their private and personal capacity. Here again the conservative policy prevailed, the Court holding that the Amendment offered no protection from individual invasion of individual rights and that Congress had no power under the Amendment to make positive and affirmative laws for its enforcement.

These two cases are landmarks in our constitutional history. They marked the practical overthrow of the Congressional ideal for the Fourteenth Amendment within seven years after its victorious adoption. The Supreme Court thus at the outset practically annulled section five of the Amendment and reduced the bill of

[1] 16 Wall. 67.
[2] U. S. *v.* Cruikshank, 92 U. S. 542.

rights of section one to distant potentialities. It denied to Congress the right to invade the province of the State Legislatures and to create a Federal code for the regulation of private rights. To exercise such authority, said the Court, "would be to make Congress take the place of State legislatures and to supersede them."[1]

This action of the Court transferred the sphere of activity under the Amendment from Congress to the forum of the Courts. In holding that it was only a potential guarantee against the invasion of certain fundamental rights by the States themselves, the practical sphere of its operation was enormously reduced. It was thus rendered peculiarly non-automatic. As a weapon of defence by a citizen against the activity of his fellow-citizens it was rendered null; as against the activity of his own State it was made ponderous and unwieldy. A person thus aggrieved could not appeal to the officers of the legislative or the executive branches of the Federal Government. He could only resort to the courts where after many months — even years — of expensive litigation, his case would reach the Supreme Court of the United States for decision. If in the long process he failed to observe all of the technical rules of legal procedure which inhere in the enforcement of a constitutional right in the Federal courts, his case would be dismissed. At each stage in the progress of his case he must, in the proper place,

[1] The Slaughter House Cases, 16 Wall. 36.

at the proper time, and in the proper manner, present his federal question. Few men have been able to employ lawyers of sufficient skill and mental acumen to meet this test.

The Supreme Court, and the public at large, thinking that the Amendment had to do only with the negro race, thought thus to render the Amendment practically inoperative. It was an admission of the failure of the Congressional plan of Reconstruction. The Court did not, however, intend to exalt its own position by thus stripping Congress of the power to enforce the Amendment. That Amendment to the Constitution brought to it unwelcomed burdens and new and grave responsibilities. On the other hand, the Court, especially in the first decades of the operation of the Amendment, consistently discouraged litigation under it. These early ideals of the scope of the Amendment held by the Court may be seen by an examination of a few of the leading cases.

In Barbier *v.* Connolly,[1] Mr. Justice Field, delivering the opinion, spoke as follows: "Neither the Amendment — broad and comprehensive as it is — nor any Amendment, was designed to interfere with the power of the State — sometimes termed its police power — to prescribe regulations to promote the health, peace, morals, education, and good order of the people, and to legislate so as to increase the industries of the State, develop its resources, and add to its wealth and pros-

[1] 113 U. S. 31.

perity." This was in 1885. A few months later, in Mo. Pac. Ry. *v.* Humes,[1] the Court said: "If the laws enacted by a State be within the legitimate sphere of legislative power, and their enforcement be attended with the observance of those general rules which our system of jurisprudence prescribes for the security of private rights, the harshness, injustice, and oppressive character of such laws will not invalidate them as affecting life, liberty, or property without due process of law. . . . This Court is not a harbor where refuge can be found from every act of ill-advised and oppressive State legislation."

In 1896, in Fallbrook Irrigation District *v.* Bradley,[2] the Court, through Mr. Justice Peckham, further elaborated this point of view in the following language: "It was never intended that the Court should, as the effect of the Amendment, be transferred into a court of appeal, where all decisions of State courts, involving merely questions of general justice and equitable considerations in the taking of property should be submitted to this Court for its determination. The final jurisdiction of the courts of the States would thereby be enormously reduced and a corresponding increase in the jurisdiction of this Court would result, and it would be a great misfortune in each case."

This attitude of the Court toward a narrow construction of the scope of the Amendment could not prevail against the steadily increasing tide of litigation which

[1] 115 U. S. 520. [2] 164 U. S. 157.

came into being by virtue of its adoption. This was due to a lack of coöperation from the members of the Bar as well as to the uncertain character of the Amendment itself, the Court having never at any time attempted its definition.

As soon as cases began to arise involving questions other than those touching the negro race, the Court entered vigorous protests. In Davidson *v.* New Orleans,[1] after a learned historical discussion of "due process of law," Mr. Justice Miller spoke for the Court as follows: "It is not a little remarkable, that while this provision has been in the Constitution of the United States as a restraint upon the authority of the Federal Government, for nearly a century, and while during all that time the manner in which the powers of the Government have been exercised has been watched with jealousy and subjected to the most rigid criticism in all of its branches, this special limitation upon its powers has rarely been invoked in the judicial forum or the more enlarged theatre of public discussion. But while it has been a part of the Constitution as a restraint upon the powers of the States, only a very few years, the docket of this Court is crowded with cases in which we are asked to hold that State Courts and State Legislatures have deprived their own citizens of life, liberty, or property without due process of law. There is here abundant evidence that there exists some strange misconception of the scope of this provision

[1] 96 U. S. 103.

as found in the Fourteenth Amendment. In fact, it would seem from the character of many of the cases before us, and the arguments made in them, that the clause under consideration is looked upon as a means of bringing to the test of the decision of this Court the abstract opinions of every unsuccessful litigant in a State court of the justice of the decision against him, and of the merits of the legislation on which such a decision may be founded."

This opinion was rendered after the Amendment had been in operation about nine years. Eight years later, in 1885, the above *dictum* was quoted verbatim by Mr. Justice Field, with the following remark: "This language was used in 1877, and now after the lapse of eight years, it may be repeated with an expression of increased surprise at the continued misconception of the purpose of the provision."[1] At the beginning of the October Term of 1877, the Supreme Court had rendered only nine opinions in cases involving the Fourteenth Amendment. From 1877 to the beginning of the October Term of 1885, twenty-six additional opinions were rendered, making a total of thirty-five for the first sixteen years of the operation of the Amendment. What would the learned Justices have said could they have foreseen the present-day operation of the Amendment! Within the last thirteen years the Supreme Court has delivered four hundred and nine opinions by way of interpreting section one of the

[1] Mo. Pac. Ry. *v.* Humes, 115 U. S. 520.

Amendment, this being an average of about thirty-one opinions each year.

In theory, the Amendment is all-embracing. Its language is comprehensive. It makes no exceptions as to the subject-matter which might come under its provisions. The attempt of the Supreme Court to limit its operation chiefly to the negro race has signally failed. The further attempt to discourage and curtail general litigation under it, also, as we have seen, met with small success.

Within recent years the Supreme Court has largely abandoned its earlier narrow interpretation of the Fourteenth Amendment. It is now given a width of scope which would have astounded the members of the Court of the seventies and eighties. What they dreaded as a misfortune has come to pass. The Amendment is now the chief source of litigation among all the provisions of the Federal Constitution. In the appellate proceedings from the States, it embraces the predominant share. In our study of the great problems which to-day confront the Nation, the Fourteenth Amendment as a constitutional factor of Federal intervention and control demands our careful consideration.

CHAPTER III

The Practical Scope of the Amendment

The Congressional programme for the scope of the Amendment came to a sudden end at the hands of the Supreme Court. Within the short period intervening its adoption and the first cases involving its interpretation, the weight of public opinion had already repudiated the governmental ideal of the Radicals. The destinies of the measure having now been left to the Supreme Court, that tribunal attempted to set forth in general terms its future sphere of activity. This was done not so much by way of positive definition as by protests against certain classes of litigation under the Amendment. This original programme of the Court has, by the logic of events, also failed.

We now turn to see what is the actual and practical scope of the Amendment, that is to say, in what manner and to what extent it operates on the States. The spheres of State activity may be classified under four heads, viz: (1) The power of eminent domain, or the taking of private property for public use after just compensation; (2) the power of taxation, through which the revenues are produced, and the free exercise of which is essential to the life of a State; (3) the police power, or power to promote the peace, happiness, health, prosperity, and general welfare of its people; and (4) the power of procedure. For lack of a better, this term is used to embrace all of those activities of the State, administrative, executive, or judicial, whereby the State seeks to enforce its laws.

The enforcement of the Fourteenth Amendment may involve a restraint, temporary or permanent, on any of the above spheres of State activity. This restraint, however, can only be exercised through the judicial branch of the Federal Government. The Amendment, under its present interpretation and methods of procedure, gives to the Supreme Court of the United States the jurisdiction to inquire into and have the final decision as to the validity of every act of a State Legislature and every proceeding of any administrative, executive, or judicial officer of the State. There are no exceptions, provided of course the party aggrieved properly presents his complaint.

The present attitude of the Supreme Court of the United States as to this question may be stated in the words of the opinion in Raymond *v.* Chicago Traction Co.,[1] decided at the October Term, 1907, viz.: "The provisions of the Fourteenth Amendment are not confined to the action of the State through its Legislature, or through the executive or judicial authority. Those provisions relate to and cover all of the instrumentalities by which the State acts, and so it has been held

[1] 207 U. S. 35, 36.

that, whoever by public position under a State government deprives another of any right protected by that Amendment against deprivation by the State, violates the constitutional inhibition." The rights protected by the Amendment are those related to the making and enforcing of laws concerning life, liberty, and property. There is the additional inhibition as to discrimination in any sphere of State activity. These rights, of course, embrace the most fundamental laws of the State, substantive and adjective.

Since the adoption of the Amendment the power of the States as to eminent domain has been questioned under it twenty-seven times, the power of taxation one hundred and forty-four times, the power of procedure one hundred and forty-six times, and the police power three hundred and two times. The bulk of these cases have arisen since 1896.[1] The total number of actual and positive Federal interventions were fifty-five, thirty-five of which imposed some positive restraint upon the police power of the States.[2]

We shall now pass in review the subject-matter of a few of these cases. Without entering into the merits of each controversy, it will suffice here merely to mention briefly the point at issue. Territorially and topically we cover a wide stretch, to wit: Suit to recover the value of a dog in Louisiana on which no tax had been paid;[3] the right of a preacher to hold

[1] See Chart, Appendix C. [2] See Chart No. II, p. 82.
[3] Sentell v. New Orleans & C. R.R. Co., 166 U. S. 698.

meetings on the Boston Common;[1] the right of a woman lawyer of the District of Columbia to practise before the courts of Virginia;[2] a suit in New York to recover damages for the illegal use of the plaintiff's photograph;[3] the sale of cigarettes in Tennessee;[4] the regulation of the height of buildings in Boston;[5] the question whether a convicted murderer in Idaho should be hanged by the sheriff or by the warden;[6] the question of the sanity of a certain man in Alabama;[7] the regulation of the practice of medicine in Michigan;[8] a consideration of the gambling laws of New York;[9] the compelling of railroads in Texas to cut the Johnson grass off from their rights of way before it goes to seed;[10] compelling the people of Massachusetts to undergo the operation of vaccination;[11] the segregation of houses of ill fame in New Orleans;[12] the question whether running a barber shop on Sunday in Minnesota is a work of necessity or the practice of a handicraft for gain;[13] the disposal of city garbage in Cali-

[1] Davis *v.* Massachusetts, 167 U. S. 43.

[2] *In re* Lockwood, 154 U. S. 116.

[3] Sperry & Hutchinson Co. *v.* Rhodes, 220 U. S. 502.

[4] Austin *v.* Tennessee, 179 U. S. 343.

[5] Williams *v.* Parker, 188 U. S. 491; Welch *v.* Swasey, 214 U. S. 91.

[6] Davis *v.* Burke, 179 U. S. 399.

[7] Simon *v.* Craft, 182 U. S. 427.

[8] Reetz *v.* Michigan, 188 U. S. 505.

[9] Adams *v.* New York, 192 U. S. 585.

[10] M. K. & T. Ry. Co. *v.* May, 194 U. S. 267.

[11] Jacobson *v.* Massachusetts, 197 U. S. 11.

[12] L'Hote *v.* New Orleans, 177 U. S. 587.

[13] Petit *v.* Minnesota, 177 U. S. 165.

fornia;[1] a consideration of the milk law of New York;[2] determining the amount of damages for a dog bite in Michigan;[3] prohibition in Nebraska of the use of the flag of the United States for the purpose of advertising;[4] the regulation of sheep grazing in Idaho;[5] the determination in Illinois of the question whether the proceedings of a trial should have been spoken through the defendant's ear trumpet;[6] reducing street car fares for the school children in Boston;[7] the labelling of mixed paints in North Dakota;[8] the selling of game in New York;[9] drumming for hotels and boarding houses on the passenger trains in Arkansas;[10] the right of women to vote in Missouri;[11] and, we mention finally, the regulation of graveyards in California![12] A motley array indeed! Yet these are but a small number of cases selected at random from the six hundred and four opinions that have been delivered by the Court under the Fourteenth Amendment.

The above cases are cited to show how the Amendment may be used to intervene in the purely local

[1] Reduction Co. *v.* Sanitary Works, 199 U. S. 306.
[2] Lieberman *v.* Van de Carr, 199 U. S. 552.
[3] Chapin *v.* Fye, 179 U. S. 127.
[4] Halter *v.* Nebraska, 205 U. S. 34.
[5] Bacon *v.* Walker, 204 U. S. 311.
[6] Felts *v.* Murphy, 201 U. S. 123.
[7] Interstate Ry. Co. *v.* Massachusetts, 207 U. S. 79.
[8] Heath Mfg. Co. *v.* Worst, 207 U. S. 338.
[9] Silz *v.* Hesterberg, 211 U. S. 31.
[10] Williams *v.* Arkansas, 217 U. S. 79.
[11] Minor *v.* Happersett, 21 Wall. 162.
[12] Cemetery Co. *v.* San Francisco, 216 U. S. 358.

affairs of a State — questions which only by the greatest stretch of the imagination can be considered as of national import. Only a very unpractical mind could conjure up a political philosophy that would hold it to be an issue of national concern whether the operating of barber shops on Sunday in Minnesota be a work of necessity or the practice of a handicraft for gain, or what damages should be given a man in Michigan when his neighbor's dog jumps through the front gate and bites him on the leg! To justify this phase of the operation of the Fourteenth Amendment would set up a theory of abstract justice which can have no justification in fact, and which has been many times repudiated by the Supreme Court itself. A people born and bred in the high ideals of liberty and independence can but resent the encroachment of this new paternalism.

It is not, however, alone with small questions that it becomes the duty of the Supreme Court to consider under the Amendment. The larger and more vital local problems of the States are also involved. We shall have occasion to treat these more fully in connection with other phases of these studies. We take occasion here simply to mention some of these questions on which the Court has rendered opinions by way of interpretation of the Amendment, to wit: State regulation of gas, water, telephone, telegraph, warehouse, and railroad rates; various city problems, such as the improvement of streets, expansion, annexation, etc.; labor laws; liquor laws; pure food laws; banking laws; insurance laws; anti-trust laws; income and inheritance tax laws; employer's liability acts; questions of court procedure and jurisdiction; and all phases of the criminal law.

Potentially the Fourteenth Amendment is of universal application as related to State activity. Its practical scope is, however, limited by the decreasing conservative attitude of the Supreme Court as well as by the legal skill and financial resources of the litigant.

CHAPTER IV

THE SOUTH

THIS chapter is here introduced as a means of calling attention to the fact that the Fourteenth Amendment to the Constitution of the United States is no longer a Southern question. Public opinion is in many respects slow and conservative. The new and living ideals of one generation become the settled dogmas of the next. What was true of certain social situations decades past is believed to be true for the present. This condition of the social mind is inevitable on those questions which are not openly agitated and those not adapted to popular investigation and discussion. The Fourteenth Amendment was in its inception purely a Southern question. In the political campaigns during the Reconstruction it was the most important issue. At that time it became firmly fixed in the public mind that the Amendment was directly related to the South and the negro and to nothing else.

The litigation which came up under the Amendment during the early years of its operation consisted largely of purely Southern questions, the Supreme Court of the United States itself declaring that this new constitutional provision had no wider scope of operation than the solution of problems arising from the presence of the negro race.

CHART NO. I

SHOWING GEOGRAPHICAL DISTRIBUTION OF LITIGATION UNDER THE AMENDMENT

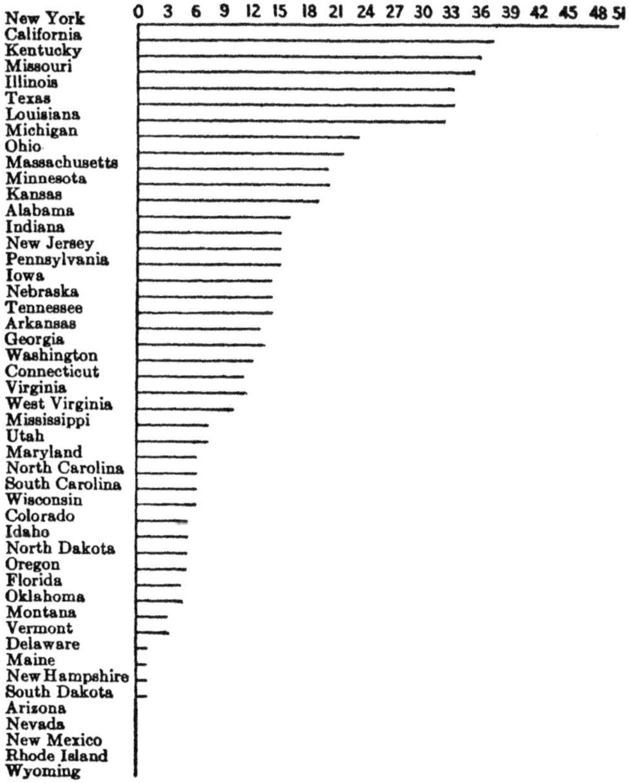

After the political excitement of the late sixties and seventies had subsided, and the country began to devote its time and attention to the more pressing economic problems of the day, the Fourteenth Amendment was lost sight of and largely forgotten by the

public. Thus to-day there is the general feeling, even among the educated classes, that the Amendment is a matter of only historical interest. They have a vague notion that it had something to do with the Civil War and slavery and that it is now of no practical concern.

The accompanying chart shows the geographical distribution of litigation under the Amendment since its adoption in 1868. The figures to the left indicate the number of opinions delivered by the Supreme Court of the United States. It will be seen, upon a close examination, that the battle-ground of the Amendment is at present in the West and the Southwest. There were one hundred and seventeen of these cases from the East, two hundred and eleven from the South, and two hundred and eighty from the West.[1] The most of these cases from the Western States have arisen within the last decade.

Twenty-eight opinions have been delivered in cases coming up from the Southern and the border States, involving the negro race question. Otherwise this entire amount of litigation partakes of the same quality, regardless of geographical location. The total number of cases coming up from the States of the East plus those from the States of the older South was two hundred and forty-three. Nearly one-third of these came

[1] This makes a total of 608. The total number of opinions was 604, but five States were represented in the Civil Rights Cases under one opinion.

up from Boston and New York City. The total from the West and the Southwest was three hundred and sixty-five. Thus the distribution of litigation under the Amendment cannot be accounted for on the basis of the density of the population. The West and the Southwest are sparsely settled, and many of their States came into the Union after the adoption of the Amendment.

This situation may, however, be partially explained. The people of the West are characterized by boldness, independence, and virility. They are impatient of restraint. Nothing could be more distasteful to them than paternalism. That country is new and of broad expanse. It stands in marked contrast to the crowded East. Its very atmosphere breeds a love of liberty of action. This inherent quality of the West may be regarded as one factor. The other is complementary thereto. About a half century ago the Federal Government gave large land grants to encourage railroad building in the West. These railroads, being thus substantially fixed to the soil, prospered. They developed into great trunk lines, owned by capitalists in the East. With the growth of population westward, other public service corporations came in their train. Within recent years they have become powerful factors, not only in the social, but also in the political, life of the West and the Southwest.

Now this lively litigation under the Fourteenth Amendment in the West may be largely accounted for as an attempt by the railroads and other public service corporations to resist the efforts of the people to control them. The hardy and vigorous Western folk stand foremost in the Nation in their attempts to throw off the control of the so-called "interests" and the powers of special privilege.

The invoking of the Amendment as a protection from State activity is more prevalent in those sections of the country where legislation and the enforcement of the laws are more vigorous and aggressive. The Amendment is being used to dispute each new step in the direction of local reforms. In this respect it concerns the South only as it concerns the Nation. It has within recent years served to complicate and intensify the great economic problems of our day, of which the South holds the lesser share. Its future field of operation will be still further enlarged in the West. Laws resulting from the current reforms in the method of government in those States will be brought to the bar of the Supreme Court of the United States by the corporations against which they are largely aimed. Wherever there is new legislation, reaching out into untried paths, its validity will be questioned under the Fourteenth Amendment.

CHAPTER V

Litigation involving the Negro Race

The presence of a large number of persons of African descent within our bounds — different in origin, temperament, and physical appearance from the Teutonic stock among whom they dwell — has ever been a serious problem in the life of our republic. The organic law of the land has more than once felt the effect of this situation, a situation abnormal in a high degree. The influence of the negro on our constitutional development, though in a large measure negative, has been none the less potent. Constitutional Law in its very nature lies closest to the life of the people. It does not originate with the political doctrinaire. It has its roots deep in the social organism. It grows and changes as the people grow and change. And so in a society of mixed races, so widely different as Teuton and African, the organic law should be expected to express this peculiar condition of life which the forces of the past have bequeathed to us. But if under these circumstances it takes into account, not a condition of life, but a theory of life, we may expect to find the life of the people failing to conform to the constitutional ideal so expressed, no matter how noble and exalted such an ideal, in the abstract, may be.

The relation of the negro race to the adoption and the interpretation of the Fourteenth Amendment to the Constitution of the United States is of profound historical and practical interest.

The Civil War had changed the legal status of the negro. The problem of readjustment to this new situation stared the country in the face. It presented a condition without a parallel in history. Under the presidential policy of reconstruction the South was gradually attempting to meet the new conditions. But Congress, under the lead of the radical wing of the Republican Party, looked upon these efforts with extreme disfavor, discredited the President, and took the entire responsibility for reconstruction into their own hands. They were led by the impractical idealist Sumner in the Senate and the partisan politician Stevens in the House. The South was excluded and had no voice in these deliberations. The Democrats of the North, in a hopeless minority, raised the voice of protest and warning, but without avail. It was the day of the Radicals. In the heat of passion and in the fervor of partisan zeal they set to work to accomplish a task which might well have engaged the most sober deliberations of the wisest heads of any people.

In these times the negro question was predominant. It was the vital element in this reconstruction legislation. It was responsible for the anomalous situation in which the country found itself at the close of the War. From 1866 to 1876 the negro race question was the keynote of every political campaign. It was uppermost in the minds of the people. The fear that the South would oppress the freedmen was the political lash by which many a voter was beaten back into the party fold.

The Fourteenth Amendment was a part of this reconstruction programme. It embodied the ideal of the Radicals. It was adopted in 1868 by ultra-radical means. It was from first to last a party measure and was fought through as such with definite party aims in view.

Although the Amendment has five sections, we are here concerned with only the first and the last, which read as follows:—

> "SECTION 1. All persons born or naturalized in the United States and subject to the jurisdiction thereof, are citizens of the United States and of the State wherein they reside. No State shall make or enforce any law which shall deprive any person of life, liberty, or property without due process of law; nor deny to any person within its jurisdiction the equal protection of the laws.
>
> "SECTION 5. The Congress shall have power to enforce, by appropriate legislation, the provisions of this article."[1]

There is here no mention of the negro as such, but it would be easy to establish from contemporaneous

[1] Proclaimed to be in effect July 28, 1868.

sources that this constitutional provision was primarily intended for the benefit of the negro race. On May 10, 1866, when the measure passed the House by a vote of 128 to 37, the applause in the galleries was loud and prolonged. "Mr. Eldridge of Wisconsin called upon the Speaker to put a stop to such proceedings. Jack Rogers hoped the colored brethren and sisters in the galleries would be allowed to wave their pocket handkerchiefs." [1] This may be regarded as one of the signs of the times. The congressional interpretation of the Amendment may be understood best by an examination of the legislation which was enacted under and by virtue of its adoption. Section five was intended to vitalize section one by giving Congress power to enact direct and positive laws for its enforcement. Pursuant to this ideal, several measures were passed, the most drastic and comprehensive of which was the Civil Rights Act of 1875. The negro question was fundamentally related to this Act. It was an attempt to lift the negro up to a plane of equality with the whites and was the chief offspring of the Fourteenth Amendment.

There were many thoughtful men of that time who shared the popular belief that the Amendment had no wider mission than that of protecting the freedmen from the so-called "Black Codes" of the Southern States. Mr. Justice Miller, in delivering the opinion

[1] *New York Herald*, May 11, 1866. Quoted by Flack, in *The Adoption of the Fourteenth Amendment.*

in the Slaughter House Cases, pronounced the following dictum: "We doubt very much whether any action of a State not directed by way of discrimination against the negroes as a class, or on account of their race, will ever be held to come within the purview of this provision." [1] During the early period of the operation of the Amendment this dictum was adhered to by the majority of the Supreme Bench. It was cited with approval and further elaborated in Strauder *v.* West Virginia,[2] in which the Court said: "This is one of a series of constitutional provisions having a common purpose; namely, securing to a race recently emancipated . . . all the civil rights that the superior race enjoy." This was the view held also by the masses of the people in so far as they understood the measure

Although this race situation may be said to have been the immediate or proximate cause of the adoption of the Amendment, as well as its immediate field of operation, in the mind of the Radicals it had a much wider scope. To them it meant the ultimate centralization of power into the hands of the Federal Government. It meant the death knell of the doctrine of States' Rights — the ultimate nationalization of all civil rights and the consequent abolition of State control over the private rights and duties of the individual.

[1] 16 Wall. 81.

[2] 100 U. S. 306. See also *Ex parte* Virginia, 100 U. S. 344, and Plessy *v.* Ferguson, 163 U. S. 537.

It meant the passing over of the police power of the State into the police power of the national government, thereby giving to Congress undefined and unlimited powers whereby it would be enabled to enter fields of legislation from which hitherto it had been barred.

These elements were not emphasized in the political campaigns from 1866 to 1868 which led up to the adoption of the Amendment. They were too intricate and subtle for the popular mind. They were, however, discerned by the leaders of the opposition, both in the North and in the South, and were combated accordingly. It is sufficient, however, for our purpose to note that in the adoption and the attempted enforcement of the Amendment by Congress, the negro race question played a prominent and controlling part. It was to be, *par excellence*, the negro's charter of liberty.

It is now forty-three years since the adoption of the Amendment. It has been in operation long enough for us to see the actual function it has performed and can perform as a part of the Supreme Law of the Land. Has it followed the course marked out by its framers? What relation has its operation had to the life of the black man in our body politic? The answer to these questions may be found in the reports of the decisions of the Supreme Court of the United States. Under the genius of our government it is here that all such questions must come for final adjudication. That answer is written large and plain. Of the six hundred and four cases involving the Fourteenth Amendment in which the Supreme Court has delivered opinions since 1868, only twenty-eight deal with questions involving the negro race; that is to say, less than five per cent of the total litigation under the Amendment. The other five hundred and seventy-six cases have to do with matters far removed from the race question. The Amendment has, in a way unforeseen by its framers, become gradually intertwined with the great economic problems which vex the country to-day. It is not the negro, but accumulated and organized capital, which now looks to the Fourteenth Amendment for protection from State activity.

A closer study of these cases but emphasizes the remoteness of the Amendment from the actual life of the problems growing out of the mixed society of African and Teuton in the United States. These it now becomes our duty to examine in some detail.

Although the Amendment was adopted and proclaimed in July, 1868, the first litigation thereunder to reach the Supreme Court of the United States was decided April 14, 1873. These are known as the Slaughter House Cases.[1] The negro question was not directly involved, but the decision proved of far-reaching consequence for that race. The chief constitutional point before the Court was the interpretation of that clause of the Amendment which reads, "No State shall make or enforce any law which shall

[1] 16 Wall. 36.

abridge the privileges or immunities of citizens of the United States." The Court decided that under our system of government there were two species of citizenship, each with it privileges and immunities — a Federal citizenship and a State citizenship. To the former were attached only such privileges or immunities as were directly due to the nature of the Federal Government and derived therefrom. All other privileges or immunities were inherent in State citizenship. The Court did not attempt to define either of these respective spheres, but it left the distinct impression that the privileges or immunities of citizens of the United States were rather few and unusual, while those attaching to State citizenship were directly related to the whole life, public and private, of the individual. In other words, the Court declared that this clause of the Amendment was not intended to interfere with the police power of the States. For the negro this means, in so far as this clause is concerned, that he must look to his State for protection rather than to the Federal Government.

We shall now briefly outline in chronological order each of the cases specifically involving the negro race question.

OCTOBER TERM, 1875

(1) U. S. *v.* Cruikshank.[1]

Cruikshank and several other white men broke up by violent means a negro political meeting in Louisiana.

[1] 92 U. S. 542.

They were arrested under section six of the Enforcement Act of May 30, 1870, tried and convicted in the Circuit Court of the United States for the District of Louisiana. On appeal to the Supreme Court they were acquitted on the ground that the Fourteenth Amendment did not justify such legislation by Congress. The citizen must not look to the Federal Government for protection against the invasion of his rights by the private acts of others. Decision against Federal intervention.

OCTOBER TERM, 1879

(2) Strauder *v.* West Virginia.[1]

Strauder, a negro, was indicted, tried, and convicted for the crime of murder in a State court. All negroes were excluded from the grand and petit juries by West Virginia Statutes of 1872–1873. The defendant contended that this was in conflict with U. S. Revised Statutes, Section 1977. This section embodied portions of the Enforcement Act of 1870 and the Civil Rights Act of 1875. Upon proceedings in the United States Supreme Court the State court was reversed and the West Virginia Act of 1872–1873 declared unconstitutional. Field and Clifford, JJ., dissented. Decision in favor of Federal intervention.

(3) Virginia *v.* Rives.[2]

Two negro men were indicted for the murder of a white man and tried in a State court before a jury composed only of white men. Defendants moved for a modification of the venire so as to allow one-third of the same to be composed of negroes. This motion was denied. Defendants then petitioned for a removal to the United States Circuit Court under the Civil Rights Act of 1875. This petition was also denied. There-

[1] 100 U. S. 303. [2] 100 U. S. 313.

upon they were tried and convicted. A petition in the United States Circuit Court for the writ of *habeas corpus* was allowed and the case docketed therein. The Commonwealth of Virginia then petitioned the Supreme Court of the United States for a writ of mandamus to compel the return of the prisoners to the custody of the State. The petition was granted on the ground that the defendants could not as a matter of right demand a mixed jury, the court declaring that the Fourteenth Amendment is not violated if, when the jury is all white, it cannot be shown that negroes were excluded solely on the ground of race or color. Decision against Federal intervention.

(4) *Ex parte* Virginia.[1]

J. D. Coles, Esq., Judge of the County Court of Pittsylvania County, Virginia, was arrested by Federal indictment in the District Court of the United States for the Western District of Virginia for failing to select negroes as grand and petit jurors to serve in the county courts of the above-mentioned county. This arrest was made under section four of the Civil Rights Act of 1875. Petitions to the Supreme Court of the United States for the writ of *habeas corpus* were filed by both Coles and the Commonwealth of Virginia. These petitions were denied and the cause remanded to the District Court for trial.

Field and Clifford, JJ., dissented. The merits of the case, that is as to whether Judge Coles was guilty of discrimination against negroes in the selection of jurymen, solely on the ground of race or color, were not involved in these proceedings. The decision went only so far as to declare section four of the Civil Rights Act of 1875 constitutional. Decision in favor of Federal intervention.

[1] 100 U. S. 339.

OCTOBER TERM, 1880

(5) Neal *v.* Delaware.[1]

The defendant, a negro, was indicted and arraigned for trial in a Delaware State court for the crime of rape upon a white woman. The Delaware Constitution of 1831, section one, article four, and the Delaware Revised Statutes of 1853, section 109, thereunder enacted, limited the selection of grand and petit jurors to the white race. On the ground of this discrimination the defendant moved to quash the indictment. This motion was denied. The defendant was thereupon tried and convicted and sentenced to be hanged. Upon a writ of error to the Delaware court the United States Supreme Court declared the law under which the juries had been drawn for the trial of the case, to be in violation of the Fourteenth Amendment and ordered the release of the prisoner. Waite, C.J., and Field, J., dissented. Decision in favor of Federal intervention.

OCTOBER TERM, 1882

(6) Pace *v.* Alabama.[2]

The defendant was tried and convicted in a State court of Alabama under Section 4189 of the Code of Alabama, which provided for a severer punishment in cases of fornication and adultery between negroes and whites than between members of the same race. Upon writ of error, the United States Supreme Court declared that this was not a denial of the equal protection of the laws under the Fourteenth Amendment. Decision against Federal intervention.

(7) Bush *v.* Kentucky.[3]

The defendant, a negro, was indicted for murder and arraigned for trial under II Revised Statutes of Ken-

[1] 103 U. S. 370. [2] 106 U. S. 583. [3] 107 U. S. 110.

tucky of 1852, p. 75, which excluded negroes from all jury service. A motion to set aside the panel of petit jurors on the ground of discrimination was overruled. Petition for removal to the United States Circuit Court was also denied. The defendant was thereupon tried, convicted, and sentenced to death. Upon writ of error, the United States Supreme Court declared the indictment void, as the law under which it was found violated the equal protection clause of the Fourteenth Amendment. Field, J., Waite, C.J., and Gray, J., dissented. Decision in favor of Federal intervention.

OCTOBER TERM, 1883

(8) The Civil Rights Cases.[1]

These were five separate causes of action, each involving the same Federal question, namely, the constitutionality of sections one and two of the Civil Rights Act of 1875. They were thus treated as one case by the United States Supreme Court. The facts may be briefly summarized as follows:—

i. The denial of hotel accommodations to certain negroes in the State of Kansas.

ii. The denial of hotel accommodations to a negro in the State of Missouri.

iii. The denial to a negro of a seat in the dress circle of Maguire's Theatre in San Francisco.

iv. The denial to a person (presumably a negro) the "full enjoyment" of the accommodations of the Grand Opera House in New York City.

v. The refusal by a conductor on a passenger train to allow a negro woman to travel in the "ladies' car" on a train of the Memphis and Charleston Railroad Company.

These acts of discrimination by private persons were severally set up as violations of sections one and two

[1] 109 U. S. 3.

of the Civil Rights Act, which, by its terms, protected the negro from the invasion of his newly given rights by the acts of private individuals as well as by action of the States. The primary question in the case was the constitutionality of this act of Congress. A further interpretation of the Thirteenth Amendment was also involved. In making the decision the court but elaborated the doctrine foreshadowed in the Slaughter House Cases [1] and formulated in United States *v.* Cruikshank,[2] and in Virginia *v.* Rives,[3] that Congress had no power under the Fourteenth Amendment to initiate direct and affirmative legislation and thus invade and destroy the police power of the States. It could only enact general laws which would regulate the enforcement of the prohibitions contained in the Amendment when they were violated by the States. It is powerless to establish a Federal Code regulating or controlling the acts of private persons in the States. Harlan, J., dissented. Decision against Federal intervention.

October Term, 1889

(9) Beatty *v.* Benton.[4]

In 1854 a negro named Carrie transferred by deed a lot in Augusta, Georgia, to a white man. Under a statute of 1818–1819, negroes could not hold real property in Georgia. Litigation over this property began in 1879 in the State courts, the outcome of which was the declaration that the deed of Carrie was void by virtue of said antebellum statute. The aggrieved party attempted to set up the Federal question that this was in contravention of the equal protection clause of the Fourteenth Amendment. Upon writ of error the United States Supreme Court decided that no Federal question

[1] 16 Wall. 36.
[2] 92 U. S. 542.
[3] 100 U. S. 313.
[4] 135 U. S. 244.

was presented, and dismissed the writ. Decision against Federal intervention.

October Term, 1894

(10) Andrews *v.* Swartz.[1]

Andrews, a negro, was indicted, tried, and convicted in a New Jersey State court for murder, and sentenced to death. He then petitioned the United States Circuit Court for a writ of *habeas corpus* on the ground that negroes had been excluded from the grand and petit juries which dealt with his case. The Circuit Court denied the petition. On appeal the Supreme Court declared that the petitioner had used the wrong method of procedure, since the regular trial of a State court cannot be reviewed by *habeas corpus* proceedings. Decision against Federal intervention.

October Term, 1895

(11) Gibson *v.* Mississippi.[2]

The defendant, a negro, was indicted for murder and arraigned in a State court. He petitioned for the removal of the cause to the Federal Court on the ground that negroes were excluded from the grand and petit juries. The petition was denied and the defendant forthwith tried and convicted. The ruling of the State court was upheld by the United States Supreme Court on writ of error. No proof was offered of discrimination against negroes "solely on the ground of race or color." Decision against Federal intervention.

(12) Charley Smith *v.* Mississippi.[3]

The defendant, a negro, was indicted for murder and arraigned in a State court for trial. He moved to quash the indictment on the ground that negroes were

[1] 156 U. S. 272. [2] 162 U. S. 565. [3] 162 U. S. 592.

excluded from the grand and petit juries. No proof of discrimination was offered. The motion was overruled and the defendant tried and convicted. Upon writ of error the United States Supreme Court affirmed the decision. Decision against Federal intervention.

(13) Murray *v.* Louisiana.[1]

The defendant, a negro, was indicted, tried, and convicted of murder by white juries. The same procedure was had as in the foregoing case. Decision against Federal intervention.

(14) Plessy *v.* Ferguson.[2]

Plessy, a person of African descent, was arrested, tried, and convicted in the Criminal District Court for the Parish of New Orleans for violating the Louisiana Statute of 1890 (No. 111, p. 152), which provided that negroes and white persons should travel in separate compartments on the passenger trains in that State. Upon proceedings had in the United States Supreme Court by way of *prohibition* and *certiorari* to test the constitutionality of said statute, it was held to be a valid exercise of the police power of the State, and therefore not in violation of the equal protection clause of the Fourteenth Amendment. Harlan, J., dissented. Decision against Federal intervention.

OCTOBER TERM, 1897

(15) Williams *v.* Mississippi.[3]

The defendant, a negro, was indicted for the crime of murder, and arraigned before juries composed entirely of white men. A motion to quash the indictment on the ground of race discrimination was overruled. A petition for removal to the United States Circuit Court

[1] 163 U. S. 101. [2] 163 U. S. 537. [3] 170 U. S. 213.

for the same alleged reason was denied. No proof of such discrimination was offered. The defendant was thereupon tried, convicted, and sentenced to death. Upon writ of error the United States Supreme Court affirmed the decision. Decision against Federal intervention.

OCTOBER TERM, 1899

(16) Cummings *v.* Board of Education.[1]

The Ware High School of Richmond County, Georgia, a public institution for negroes only, was suspended "for economic reasons," while the high school for whites in the same county was continued in operation. Cummings, a negro taxpayer, complained of discrimination against the negroes as being in violation of the "privileges and immunities" and the "equal protection" clauses of the Fourteenth Amendment. The trial did not show any abuse of discretion allowed by law to the county Board of Education. The constitutionality of all laws providing separate accommodations for whites and blacks in the public schools of the States was attacked in the argument of counsel, but the question was not presented in the record. Upon writ of error the United States Supreme Court affirmed the decision of the Supreme Court of Georgia upholding the action of the county Board of Education. Decision against Federal intervention.

(17) Carter *v.* Texas.[2]

The defendant, a negro, was indicted and arraigned in a State court for trial for the crime of murder. He moved to quash the indictment on the ground that negroes were excluded from the grand jury on account of their race or color. He offered to introduce proof in

[1] 175 U. S. 528. [2] 177 U. S. 442.

support of this motion. The court refused to allow the introduction of proof and overruled the motion. The defendant was forthwith tried and convicted. Upon writ of error the United States Supreme Court reversed the decision of the State court and remanded the case on the ground that the trial court erred in refusing to receive proof in support of said motion. Decision in favor of Federal intervention.

October Term, 1902

(18) Tarrance *v.* Florida.[1]

The defendant, a negro, was indicted and arraigned for trial for the crime of murder. The juries were composed entirely of white men. He moved to quash the indictment on the ground of racial discrimination. No proof was offered in support of the motion. He was forthwith tried and convicted. Upon writ of error the United States Supreme Court affirmed the decision of the State court. Decision against Federal intervention.

(19) Brownfield *v.* South Carolina.[2]

The defendant, a negro, was indicted for the crime of murder before a grand jury composed entirely of white men. He moved to quash the indictment because of an alleged exclusion of negroes therefrom on account of their race or color. The motion further set up that the negroes constituted four-fifths of the population of the county. No proof of discrimination was offered. The defendant was tried and convicted and the proceedings of the State court were affirmed, upon writ of error, by the United States Supreme Court. Decision against Federal intervention.

[1] 188 U. S. 519. [2] 189 U. S. 426.

(20) Giles *v.* Harris.[1]

Giles, a negro, instituted proceedings to test the constitutionality of the suffrage clauses of the Constitution of Alabama of 1901. The interpretation of the Fifteenth Amendment was the paramount issue, although the "equal protection" clause of the Fourteenth Amendment was involved. An adverse decision was given in the State courts. The defendant prosecuted a writ of error to the Supreme Court of Alabama, which was dismissed for want of jurisdiction by the United States Supreme Court. The record did not present a Federal question. Brewer, Brown, and Harlan, JJ., dissented. Decision against Federal intervention.

OCTOBER TERM, 1903

(21) Rogers *v.* Alabama.[2]

The defendant, a negro, was indicted and arraigned for the crime of murder. The juries were composed entirely of white men. He moved to quash the indictment on the ground that negroes were excluded from the juries on account of their race or color. The motion was stricken from the files for prolixity and the defendant tried and convicted. Upon writ of error the United States Supreme Court decided that the motion was relevant, properly presented a Federal question, and, though perhaps including some superfluous matter, should not have been stricken from the files on the ground of local practice. Proof should have been allowed to have been introduced under the motion. The State court was reversed and the cause remanded. Decision in favor of Federal intervention.

(22) Giles *v.* Teasley.[3]

This was a second attempt by Giles, a negro, to test the constitutionality of the suffrage clauses of the Consti-

[1] 189 U. S. 475. [2] 192 U. S. 226. [3] 193 U. S. 146.

tution of Alabama of 1901. The Fifteenth Amendment, as before, was predominantly involved, the Fourteenth being only of secondary importance. The case was decided adversely in the State courts. Upon writ of error the United States Supreme Court dismissed the proceedings on the ground that the record did not present a Federal question. The pleadings of the plaintiff were inconsistent, one allegation neutralizing the other. Harlan, J., dissented. Decision against Federal intervention.

October Term, 1905

(23) Martin *v.* Texas.[1]

The defendant, a negro, was indicted for the crime of murder and arraigned for trial. He moved to quash the indictment on the ground that all negroes had been excluded from the grand and petit juries because of race or color. No proof of discrimination was offered. The motion was overruled and the defendant tried, convicted, and sentenced to death. The United States Supreme Court, upon writ of error, reiterated its former opinions that the defendant could not, as a matter of right, demand a mixed jury. Decision against Federal intervention.

October Term, 1906

(24) Hodges *v.* United States.[2]

Hodges and several other white men were indicted by a grand jury in the District Court of the United States for the Eastern District of Arkansas on the charge of threatening and intimidating eight negro laborers in a certain lumber yard. The indictment was found under U. S. Revised Statutes, Sections 1977–

[1] 200 U. S. 316. [2] 203 U. S. 81

1999, 5508 and 5510, which embodied portions of the Civil Rights Act of 1866, the Enforcement Act of 1870, the Ku Klux Act of 1871, and the Civil Rights Act of 1875. The interpretation of all three of the War Amendments was involved, the Thirteenth being predominant. The defendants demurred to the indictment as presenting no Federal question. This was overruled and the defendants forthwith tried and convicted. Upon writ of error the Supreme Court reversed the District Court and remanded the cause with instructions to sustain the demurrer. The alleged offence having been committed by private persons was not within the jurisdiction of a Federal court. Harlan and Day, JJ., dissented. Decision against Federal intervention.

October Term, 1908

(25) Berea College *v.* Kentucky.[1]

Berea College, a Kentucky corporation, was indicted under section one of the Acts of Kentucky of 1904, Chap. 85, which provided that no person or corporation should operate any school or college in which persons of the white and the negro races were both received as pupils. The facts were undisputed, Berea College being such a mixed school. The only point in the case was the constitutionality of the above-mentioned law under the Fourteenth Amendment. The trial in the State court resulted in a conviction and fine. Upon being brought to the United States Supreme Court by writ of error, the case turned upon the point that the defendant was a corporation and not a person, and hence being a creature of the State was subject to its control in this particular. The question as to the power of the State to enforce the separation of the races in schools *per se* was not decided. Only that

[1] 211 U. S. 45.

portion of the Act which referred to the restrictions on corporations was declared constitutional. The Supreme Court — like other forces — follows the line of least resistance. If a case be disposed of on a lesser point, the greater will not be decided. One cannot but admire the logic and ultimate justice of such a rule. Harlan, J., dissented. Decision against Federal intervention.

(26) Thomas *v.* Texas.[1]

The defendant, a negro, was indicted and arraigned on the charge of murder. He moved to quash the indictment on the ground that all negroes had been excluded from the grand and petit juries. No proof of discrimination was offered. The motion was overruled and the defendant tried, convicted, and sentenced to death. Upon writ of error the United States Supreme Court affirmed the decision of the State court on the ground aforementioned that discrimination will not be presumed. Decision against Federal intervention.

OCTOBER TERM, 1909

(27) Marbles *v.* Creecy.[2]

A requisition was issued by the Governor of Mississippi to the Governor of Missouri for the return of Marbles, a negro, who was charged with the crime of assault with intent to murder. He had fled to the State of Missouri. Upon being arrested in the latter State, by virtue of said requisition, he petitioned for a writ of *habeas corpus* in the United States Circuit Court, setting up the alleged fact that it was not possible that he could receive a fair trial should he be returned to the State of Mississippi, on account of his race or color. No proof was offered that such a state of affairs would

[1] 212 U. S. 278. [2] 215 U. S. 63.

come to pass. The petition was denied by the Circuit Court. Upon appeal to the United States Supreme Court the decision was affirmed and the prisoner ordered to be surrendered. Decision against Federal intervention.

(28) Franklin *v.* South Carolina.[1]

Pink Franklin, a negro, shot and killed one Valentine, a constable, who was attempting to arrest him for the violation of a certain South Carolina statute. He was indicted for murder, tried, convicted, and sentenced to death. No negroes were on the juries. At the trial a motion was made to quash the indictment on this ground. No statement of race discrimination was made and no proof of such discrimination offered. Upon writ of error the Supreme Court of the United States affirmed the judgment of the State Court. Decision against Federal intervention.

These cases deal chiefly with the matter of the enforcement of the criminal laws of the Southern States. They stand out in striking contrast to the other phases of litigation under the Amendment both as to their infrequency and the character of questions involved.

[1] 218 U. S. 161.

CHAPTER VI

Results to the Negro Race

We may now consider what phases of the negro race question have become related to the operation of the Fourteenth Amendment since its adoption in 1868. In so doing it is well to bear in mind two facts: First, that the negro race has increased in numbers during the last forty years from nearly five[1] to about ten millions, and that the social complexity of the Afro-Teutonic situation has become intensified rather than diminished. Second, that litigation under the Fourteenth Amendment has steadily increased until within recent years it has engaged the attention of the Supreme Court of the United States more than has any other part of the Constitution, with the possible exception of the Interstate Commerce clause.

An analysis of the foregoing data reveals the fact that the negro race question has been presented to the Supreme Court under this Amendment in only eight different aspects, of varying degrees of importance. They may be stated as follows: —

(1) The power of Congress to initiate under the Amendment direct and positive legislation in behalf of

[1] The negro population by the census of 1870 was 4,880,009; by the census of 1910 it was 9,828,294.

the negro as such. This had been attempted under the Enforcement Act of May 30, 1870, the Ku Klux Act of April 20, 1871, and the Civil Rights Act of February 27, 1875. This point was three times presented to the Supreme Court: once in 1875,[1] once in 1883,[2] and once as late as 1906.[3]

(2) The validity of a deed executed by a negro in Georgia in 1854, when by virtue of a Georgia statute of 1818–1819 negroes could not hold real property in that State. No Federal question was presented.[4]

(3) *Habeas corpus* proceedings to prevent the return by extradition of a negro from the State of Missouri to the State of Mississippi on the ground of probable race discrimination at the forthcoming trial in the latter State.[5]

(4) Two unsuccessful attacks by the same party on the suffrage clauses of the Constitution of Alabama of 1901. The Fifteenth Amendment was the predominant issue.[6]

(5) The power of a State to impose a severer penalty in the case of adultery between negroes and whites than for the same crime between members of the same race.[7] Code of Alabama, 1880, Section 4189.

[1] U. S. *v.* Cruikshank, 92 U. S. 542.

[2] The Civil Rights Cases, 109 U. S. 3.

[3] Hodges *v.* U. S., 203 U. S. 1.

[4] Beatty *v.* Benton, 135 U. S. 244.

[5] Marbles *v.* Creecy, 215 U. S. 63.

[6] Giles *v.* Harris, 189 U. S. 475; Giles *v.* Teasley, 193 U. S. 146.

[7] Pace *v.* Alabama, 106 U. S. 583.

(6) The power of a State to require negroes and whites to travel in separate coaches or compartments on passenger trains.[1] Louisiana Statute, 1890, No. 111, popularly known as the Jim Crow Law.

(7) The color line in education. This has been presented to the Court in two aspects, namely: The power of a State, through the discretionary authority of its county officials, to suspend a negro high school while continuing to operate the high school for whites.[2] Secondly, the power of a State to penalize an incorporated college for operating an institution in which both white and black pupils were received.[3]

(8) The exclusion of negroes from the grand and petit juries in the State courts. This phase of the question has been presented to the Supreme Court sixteen times.[4] In fourteen of these the defendant had been convicted of murder and in one of rape.

These eight groups of cases under the Fourteenth

[1] Plessy *v.* Ferguson, 163 U. S. 537.

[2] Cummings *v.* Board of Education, 175 U. S. 528.

[3] Berea College *v.* Kentucky, 211 U. S. 45.

[4] Strauder *v.* West Virginia, 100 U. S. 303 (1879); Virginia *v.* Rives, 100 U. S. 313 (1879); *ex parte* Virginia, 100 U. S. 339 (1879); Neal *v.* Delaware, 103 U. S. 370 (1880); Bush *v.* Kentucky, 107 U. S. 110 (1882); Andrews *v.* Swartz, 156 U. S. 212 (1894); Murray *v.* Louisiana, 163 U. S. 101 (1895); Gibson *v.* Mississippi, 162 U. S. 565 (1895); Charley Smith *v.* Mississippi, 162 U. S. 592 (1895); Williams *v.* Mississippi, 170 U. S. 213 (1897); Carter *v.* Texas, 177 U. S. 442 (1899); Tarrance *v.* Florida, 188 U. S. 519 (1902); Brownfield *v.* South Carolina, 189 U. S. 426 (1902); Rogers *v.* Alabama, 192 U. S. 226 (1903); Martin *v.* Texas, 200 U. S. 316 (1905); Thomas *v.* Texas, 212 U. S. 278 (1908).

Amendment are clearly of unequal importance and bear different relations to the actual problem incident to the presence of the negro race in our midst. The cases of the first group are now only of historical interest and bear no relation to the present situation. That avenue of activity under the Amendment has long been closed. The second and third groups containing one case each may be regarded as frivolous attempts at Federal intervention and may also be dismissed from consideration so far as the modern problem is concerned. Group four gains significance chiefly in relation to an alleged violation of the Fifteenth Amendment.

The remaining four groups come nearer to the real life of the races and express something of the conditions confronting them, involving as they do the following problems: Penalizing crime between the two races more heavily than between members of the same race; the color line in education; the Jim Crow Law; and the excluding of negroes from jury service. The chief phase of the Amendment which these questions involve is the clause which provides that no State shall "deny to any person within its jurisdiction the equal protection of the laws."

What may we say, then, has been the effect of the operation of the Amendment upon that race chiefly for whose benefit it was adopted? What has been its relationship to the Federal Government, what restraint has been placed upon the States, and lastly, what has it accomplished in positive results for the negro race?

As we have seen, the idea was quite prevalent at the time of the adoption of the Amendment, that its chief field of operation would be effective by virtue of direct, positive, and primary legislation by Congress in behalf of the negro race. In pursuance of this constitutional ideal, Congress began to legislate in this direction. The United States Supreme Court at an early stage of the operation of the Amendment declared all such legislation unconstitutional and beyond the power of the Federal Government. As a consequence the relationship of Congress to the Amendment has been for a long time clearly understood. It may be summed up as follows: The first section of the Amendment is a prohibitory measure, and the prohibitions therein expressed operate against the States only. They bear no relationship to the acts of private persons within the States. Section five goes only so far as to give Congress the power by general legislation to enforce these prohibitions. Congress may, within bounds, provide the modes of redress when a State has violated the prohibitions. Congress cannot enforce them against the States. The State must take the initiative in violating the Amendment; then, and then only, can the aggrieved party seek redress. And this not by an appeal to national laws, but by the complex, uncertain, and tortuous path through the courts of his State to the Supreme Court of the United States. Congress is limited to the matter of regulating the time, manner, and occasion of this appeal to Federal authority for intervention. We see, therefore, that so far as the negro question is related to the Amendment, Congress may be eliminated as a vital factor. The Supreme Court is the only branch of the Federal Government which is competent to deal with the question, and that under conditions which render the Federal Government a minimum force in the practical solution of the negro race problem. So far as the Fourteenth Amendment is concerned, the Federal Government would be powerless to prevent armed mobs of whites from driving negroes out from a State, or otherwise threatening or intimidating them in their attempt to exercise the privileges of citizenship.

We next turn to consider in what manner and to what extent has the Supreme Court sustained or rejected petitions for Federal intervention in behalf of the negro race under the operation of the Amendment. As has been shown, there were twenty-eight such appeals to Federal authority. Twenty-two of these were decided adversely to the party aggrieved. The remaining six were decided in favor of Federal intervention to a limited extent.

The police power of a State to deal with the race question has been squarely before the Supreme Court only four times within the past forty years. One of these deals with the relation of the negro to the jury system. This we shall consider later. The definite results of the other three decisions involve only two principles, to wit: (1) A State has the power to inflict a severer punishment for the crime of adultery and fornication between negroes and whites than it inflicts for the same crime between members of the same race.[1] This involves the important principle of making distinctions in law on the ground of race or color. It violates no clause of the Fourteenth Amendment. To what extent this principle may be applied to the present situation has yet to appear. (2) A State has the power to separate the races one from the other in its school systems and on the passenger trains passing through its territory. As to the first, that of maintaining separate schools for black and white, the question as such has never been clearly before the Supreme Court and has, therefore, never been decided absolutely. In Cummings *v.* Board of Education[2] the question was discussed, but the record necessitated only that the Court decide that a State may, under certain circumstances, suspend temporarily a negro high school while continuing to operate the white high school in the same locality. In rendering the opinion of the Court, however, Mr. Justice Harlan pronounced the following dictum: "The education of the people in schools maintained by State taxation is a matter belonging to the respective States, and any interference on the part of Federal authority with the management of such schools cannot be justified except in the case of a clear and unmistakable disregard of rights secured by the supreme law of the land. We have here no such case to be determined."

[1] Pace *v.* Alabama, 106 U. S. 583. [2] 175 U. S. 528.

In Berea College *v.* Kentucky[1] the question was fairly presented, but the case turned on the point that Berea College was a corporation created by the laws of Kentucky and therefore subject to the exercise of the police power of that State.

This principle of separation of African and Teuton on racial grounds is the same whether it be the maintaining of separate schools, separate churches, separate hotels, separate compartments in public conveyances, segregation in certain quarters — residential or business — of towns and cities, in the park and playground systems of the larger cities, in the theatres and other places of public amusement; in fine, the separation of the races at all times, in all places, and under all circumstances where they would in large numbers come into physical contact the one with the other.

In the case of Plessy *v.* Ferguson[2] this principle was for the first and only time properly presented to the Supreme Court of the United States for adjudication under the Fourteenth Amendment. As we have seen, the Court decided that a State has the power to require the separation of the negroes and the whites from each other on the ground of race or color in the matter of riding on passenger trains. But in rendering the majority opinion, Mr. Justice Brown further elaborated this principle of race separation, using among others the following expressions: "Legislation is powerless to eradicate racial instincts or to abolish distinctions

[1] 211 U. S. 45.

[2] 163 U. S. 537 (Louisiana).

based upon physical differences, and the attempt to do so can only result in accentuating the difficulties of the present situation. . . . If one race be inferior to the other socially, the Constitution of the United States cannot put them upon the same plane."[1] The learned Justice here struck at the root of the matter. He tacitly recognized two elements in the problem of extreme interest — the futility of the early Congressional ideal of the scope and of the efficiency of the Amendment; and the "difficulties of the present situation."

In the same opinion, after reviewing the decision in the Slaughter House Cases, he speaks as follows: "The object of the Amendment was undoubtedly to enforce the absolute equality of the races before the law, but in the nature of things it could not have been intended to abolish distinctions based upon color, or to enforce social, as distinguished from political, equality, or the commingling of the two races upon terms unsatisfactory to either. Laws permitting, and even requiring, their separation in places where they are liable to be brought into contact do not necessarily imply the inferiority of either race to the other, and have been generally, if not universally, recognized as within the competency of State legislatures in the exercise of their police power. The most common instance of this is connected with the establishment of separate schools for white and colored children, which has been

[1] 163 U. S. 544.

held to be a valid exercise of the legislative power — even by courts of States where the political rights of the colored race have been longest and most earnestly enforced."[1] Here the learned Justice cites several cases from various States of the Union and quotes from one Massachusetts case *in extenso*.[2]

This decision has been quoted at some length because it is the only instance of the Supreme Court having passed upon this vital question, and settled, it seems, once for all the principle of race separation in its relationship to the Fourteenth Amendment. The opinion enunciates sound principles of political science and is justified by the logic of history and of fact.

There seems to be no limit to which a State may go in requiring the separation of the races. May it not do on a larger what it can do on a smaller scale? So long as the law operated equally on both races, could Federal intervention under the Fourteenth Amendment be invoked by either? The situation is a strange one in a government dedicated to the most exalted ideals of democracy. It is none the less inevitable, and the operation of this principle of race separation may yet prove the means of a solution of this problem with the least injustice to white or black.

It has been in reference to the right of negroes to sit

[1] 163 U. S. 544.

[2] Roberts *v.* City of Boston, 5 Cush. 198. Separate schools for negroes and whites were maintained in Boston. The plaintiff, through his counsel, Mr. Charles Sumner, attacked the validity of the law. The Court decided against plaintiff.

on juries in the State courts that the authority of the State has been most seriously questioned. On this point alone the Federal Government has intervened in behalf of the negro race and restrained, in some measure, the action of the States. Of the sixteen cases before the Supreme Court on this question, six were decided adversely to the States involved. The sum of these decisions may be stated in a very few principles, namely: —

(1) No State can make any law which *prima facie* excludes negroes from jury service because they are negroes. Such a law would be clearly in violation of the Amendment. Only one such law has been called in question as having been enacted since July 28, 1868, the date of the adoption of the Amendment, viz.: West Virginia Acts, 1872–1873, p. 102, which limited jury service to white men.[1] On two other occasions surviving antebellum laws excluding negroes from jury service have been declared unconstitutional, to wit: Section 1, Article 4, of the Delaware Constitution of 1831,[2] and Revised Statutes of Kentucky of 1852 (pp. 75, 77).[3] It may be of interest to notice that these three cases did not come from former seceding States.

(2) No State may, through its executive, administrative, or judicial officers, exclude from jury service

[1] Strauder *v.* West Virginia, 100 U. S. 303.
[2] Neal *v.* Delaware, 103 U. S. 370.
[3] Bush *v.* Kentucky, 107 U. S. 110.

persons of African descent "solely on the ground of race or color." Three times here also the Supreme Court has intervened in behalf of the negroes. Once in 1879, when a county judge in Virginia was accused of making such discrimination.[1] This was, however, a proceeding by way of *habeas corpus*, and the merits of the alleged discrimination were not decided. In the other two instances of Federal intervention, once in 1899[2] and once in 1903,[3] the State courts were reversed on the ground that the trial court erred in refusing to receive proof of the alleged racial discrimination under a motion to quash the indictment for that reason. In other words, these three adverse decisions involved only the technicalities of legal procedure. In none of these sixteen attempts to force the States to summon negroes for jury service was there any proof of discrimination had in open court.

One other thing must be borne in mind. These cases represent no movement on the part of the negro race to obtain places on white juries. They stretch over a period of forty years. They bear no relationship to the ideals of the better element of the negro race. They come chiefly from the lower South, where there are practically no negro lawyers. These appeals to the Federal Government are the work of white attorneys, representing, through appointment or choice, poor and

[1] *Ex parte* Virginia, 100 U. S. 339.
[2] Carter *v.* Texas, 177 U. S. 442.
[3] Rogers *v.* Alabama, 192 U. S. 226.

ignorant negro criminals already convicted before State tribunals of the darkest crimes known to man. It is the grasp of the drowning man after a straw, since the invocation of the Fourteenth Amendment in the Supreme Court of the United States means that the day of execution will be delayed.

What, then, is the situation to-day in reference to this question of jury service? The principle which has been evolved out of these attempts to invoke the aid of the Federal Government under the Fourteenth Amendment may be stated negatively as follows: Where there is no discrimination in the laws of the State against negroes on the ground of race or color and where the jurors of said State are customarily all white men, discrimination against such negroes, *solely on the ground of race or color*, will not be presumed, but must be substantiated by positive proof by the party aggrieved. The Amendment can give no further guarantee than this. The effect of the operation of this principle is that practically no negroes are chosen for jury service, especially in those States where they are present in large numbers.

Since the State may exclude negroes on any ground except that of race or color, it is practically impossible for a negro to prove on what ground he has been excluded. Even though the race element entered into the motive for exclusion and formed the dominant element thereof, the discrimination would be legal under the decisions of the Supreme Court. Should we, for example, even suppose that negroes were excluded from jury service solely because of their race or color, how could the exact quality of the discrimination be proven? The difficulty is inherent. The motives of the county officers in selecting persons for jury service are too subtle, too subjective, to admit of positive proof.

We have now answered the question as to what effect the operation of the Fourteenth Amendment has had on the States in relation to the negro race problem. We have seen that no actual and practical restraint has been put upon the States in any instance where the State action was brought in question. What elements of potential restraint the Amendment has imposed or now imposes upon the States in this particular, remains a matter of speculation. How far a State may go in the attempt to apply a practical solution to the negro problem also remains to be seen. So far they have not been checked by the Federal Government. In the broad day of an enlightened public opinion, world-wide in its reach, it is not probable that backward steps will be taken. New acquisitions from the growing social and biological sciences are bringing to us a clearer and a saner point of view than that evolved from the philosophy and theology of the past generation.

In conclusion we may ask what positive gain has the operation of the Fourteenth Amendment been to the negro race? We can point to nothing. All attempts at Federal intervention have been fruitless in permanent results. The operation of the Amendment in its relation to the negro race has in it all of the irony of history. It is the perversion of a noble idealism that the lowest and most benighted element of the African race should in these enlightened days be the ones to rise up and claim the sacred heritage of Anglo-Saxon liberties which, through the fortune of circumstance, have become embodied in the Supreme Law of the Land in the shape of the Fourteenth Amendment.

But, it may be said, the Amendment is the negro's Magna Charta — it is to him a perpetual guarantee of protection from discrimination. We have seen, however, that the validity of this assertion is reduced to an uncertain and undefined minimum by the facts. If it be his charter of liberty, it is indeed a strange one. In what respect does it protect him from his State? He does not know. Unlike the charters of other people, it was written there not by his efforts nor dictated at his command. It speaks to him a strange and far-off language. It has not come and dwelt with him, because it belongs not to his world. It is spending its force in other fields to which the negro is perforce a stranger.

The words "citizen," "life, liberty, and property," "due process of law," and "the equal protection of the laws," were born through a travail in which the African had no share. They breathe the sacred symbols of a race which paid the price for greatness. They are the fruit of unmeasured sacrifice and suffering, of innumerable and lengthened struggles through defeat and failure to final victory. They are the key-words of that race which has, among all of the peoples of the earth, shown the highest genius for law and government. They can never be superimposed from without. The great truths which they embody can come into being only through the birth pangs of the inner life.

The Fourteenth Amendment declared the negro to be a citizen of the United States of America. This may, in the abstract, be considered a great advantage. But it is a serious matter to be a citizen of a country like the United States. Its ideals of citizenship presuppose centuries of independent personal and racial achievement. It looks for a soil out of which it is possible for democracy to spring. In the words of an eminent statesman and patriot: "It throws upon him a great responsibility and expects of him a constant and watchful independence. There is no one to look out for his rights but himself. He is not a ward of the government, but his own guardian. The law is not automatic; he must himself put it into operation, and he must show good cause why the courts should exercise the great powers vested in them. . . . In England, as in America, the individual citizen is bidden to take care of himself, not only against his neighbor, but also, if he can, against the government." [1]

These remarks were spoken to white men. They refer to white citizens. They give voice to one of the

[1] Woodrow Wilson, *Constitutional Government in the United States*, pp. 150, 151.

most profound principles of English and American government. Yet they apply also to the Afro-American. They speak to him with redoubled force. They set before him the most exalted ideal of citizenship yet achieved by man and bid him reach it if he can. There is a touch of pathos in all of this. The negro has been the only innocent party in this turmoil of the times. He at least, by every moral law, has been entitled to have justice meted out to him. On the contrary he has been used as a tool first by one section of the country, then by the other. He has served only the purposes of the controlling element of the stronger race. And finally, to satisfy the political idealism and the partisan plans of those to whom he himself was a stranger, he has been thrown naked, penniless, and deserted upon the land to pick his way in the midst of the highest and most complicated civilization known to the earth.

The adoption of the Fourteenth Amendment could not make Anglo-Saxons out of Africans. It was unjust to the negro to force him to play a rôle for which by the forces of nature he was unfitted. He deserves neither ridicule nor blame for the comedy and the tragedy of the Reconstruction. It is one of the fundamental precepts of political science to-day that only those people in a community can participate equally in its civic, social, and political life who are conscious of a common origin, share a common idealism, and look forward to a common destiny. Where the community is composed of two divergent races rendering such a community of life impossible, the weaker and less favored race must inevitably and in the nature of things take the place assigned to it by the stronger and dominant race. The Republican Party, which controlled all branches of the government after the War, might have made the negroes wards of the nation, putting them intc a position similar to that occupied by the American Indians. They, especially at that time, needed the protecting arm of the Federal Government thrown around them. Under this system of sympathetic tutelage the African might have been led to develop whatever latent powers that may be inherent in his race. To-day he can truly raise the cry that many of the doors of opportunity are closed to him.

As it now stands, the negro must look to his State for protection. He must take his chances along with the other citizens. If in the unequal struggle he fails to gain for himself the full fruits of citizenship, there is no recourse left to him. The strongest point in his favor is that he is human and his long sojourn in the midst of a naturally kind-hearted people has brought about certain tacit understandings and adjustments, the written Constitution to the contrary notwithstanding.

CHAPTER VII

Federal Intervention

It is not the purpose of this chapter to enter into a discussion of the philosophy of the relation of the States to the Federal Government, nor to give an exhaustive treatment of the cases here cited. It is proposed to show in outline the development and trend of the operation of the Fourteenth Amendment in its direct and positive restraint upon the several States within the past forty-three years. The attempt is made to set forth the different spheres of State activity affected and the various classes of laws which have been annulled in whole or in part.

From the time of the adoption of the Fourteenth Amendment in 1868 to the close of its last term, the Supreme Court of the United States has handed down six hundred and four opinions under that article of the Constitution. Of these applications for Federal intervention by way of restraining or annulling State action, only fifty-five were decided adversely to the States — that is to say, about nine per cent.

The accompanying chart reveals something of the history and the trend of these instances of intervention.

CHART No. II

CHRONOLOGICAL TABLE SHOWING THE NUMBER AND CHARACTER OF FEDERAL INTERVENTIONS UNDER THE FOURTEENTH AMENDMENT, 1868–1911

U. S. Supreme Court, October Term.	Number of interventions.	State Constitutions affected.	Statutes affected.	City ordinances affected.	State procedure restrained.	State court reversed.	Federal injunction sustained.	Commerce clause of U. S. Const. involved.	Other clauses of U. S. Const. involved.	Merits not decided.	Dissenting opinions.	Private corporation the principal party.	Negro race question involved.	Clauses of the Amendment at issue.		Sphere of State activity affected.		
														Equal protection of the laws.	Due process of law.	Police power.	Taxation.	Eminent domain.
1879 . . .	2		1		1	1				1	2		2		2	2		
1880 . . .	1	1				1					1		1		1	1		
1882 . . .	1		1			1					1		1		1	1		
1885 . . .	2				2	2				1		1		1	2	1	1	
1889 . . .	1		1			1			1		1	1		1	1	1		
1893 . . .	2		1		1	1	1		1			1		2		2		
1896 . . .	4		4			4			1		1	4		4	2	4		
1897 . . .	2	1	2			1	1		2			2		2	1	2		
1898 . . .	3		1	2		2	1		1		2	1		3	1	1	1	1
1899 . . .	3		1		2	2	1			2	1	1	1	2	2	3		
1900 . . .	1		1	1						1		1			1		1	
1901 . . .	2		2				1				1	2			2	2		
1902 . . .	2		1			1	1		1		1	2		2	1	1	1	
1903 . . .	3		1	1	1	3		1	1		1	2	1	1	2	2	1	
1904 . . .	6		4	1		5	1		2	1	5	4		6		3	1	2
1905 . . .	2		1	1		1	1		1	1	1	2		1	1	1	1	
1906 . . .	3		1	1	2	2	1		2		1	2		3		1	1	1
1907 . . .	4	1	3	1		2	2	1			3	3		4	1	2	2	
1908 . . .	3	1			2	2	1	2			1	2		3	1	2	1	
1909 . . .	6		5			4	2	3			6	6		5	3	1	5	
1910 . . .	2		1	1			2	1		1	2	2		2		2		
Total . .	55	4	32	9	11	36	16	8	13	8	31	39	6	42	25	35	16	4

Prior to 1885 there were four such cases, each of which involved the negro race question. These grew out of the problems of the Reconstruction. Since 1886 there have been only two cases of intervention on matters relating to the negro race, while every other instance except twelve has been in behalf of a private corporation seeking relief from State activity, to wit: thirty-nine cases.

For this entire period of forty-three years Federal intervention under the Amendment has affected four State constitutions, thirty-two statutes, and nine city ordinances, and State procedure — administrative, executive, or judicial — has been restrained eleven times. Thirty-six of these cases reached the Supreme Court of the United States by writ of error to the State court, sixteen by appeal from injunctions in the inferior Federal courts, and three by other appeals from the Federal courts. Within the past five years nearly one-half of the cases of Federal intervention have been by the way of Federal injunctions. Out of the total number of cases of intervention, twenty-one involved the interpretation of some other clause of the Constitution, eight of these being the commerce clause. In eight cases the merits were left undecided, and in thirty-one — a little over one-half — there were dissenting opinions.

It is apparent that all of these cases are not of equal importance. Some of them involve the technicalities of legal procedure. Others deal with questions no longer alive in the body politic. Others annul statutes and declare principles of prime importance. While the total number of interventions is not significant as compared with the total number of opinions handed down, yet their effect has been far-reaching on the relations of the States to the Federal Government. The restraining of the activity of one State lays down in some measure the metes and bounds for the other States. Social and economic movements involving several States have been thus checked in their incipiency.

Let us now pass to a more definite consideration of these instances of intervention with a view of seeing more clearly this phase of the practical operation of the Amendment. We shall consider first certain miscellaneous cases of more or less importance, but which represent isolated instances of Federal intervention. We shall then proceed to study the more important groups.

1. *Presumption of death.* Under probate procedure in the State of Washington, a certain man having been absent from the State for seven years, and whose whereabouts were unknown, was declared to be dead, and letters of administration were issued. He subsequently reappeared and brought suit in ejectment to recover the land. An adverse decision having been rendered by the State courts, upon writ of error, the Supreme Court of the United States declared such action of the State violative of the due process clause of the Fourteenth Amendment.[1]

[1] Scott *v.* McNeal, 154 U. S. 34. October Term, 1893.

2. *Service of process.* A Texas court served process on a defendant in Virginia, summoning him to appear in the Texas court within five days. This action was upheld by the Supreme Court of Texas. Upon writ of error the Supreme Court of the United States declared the notice insufficient as depriving the defendant of due process of law in contravention of the Fourteenth Amendment.[1] Fuller, C.J., and Brewer, J., dissented.

3. *Eminent domain.* (*a*) Procedure in Kentucky to condemn certain lands for a right of way.[2] On the ground of the non-residence of the defendant, and under the due process of law clause of the Fourteenth Amendment, the case was removed to the Federal court. A Federal injunction was thenceforth issued to restrain further proceedings in the State court. On appeal the Supreme Court of the United States upheld the injunction. The merits of the case were not decided.[3] Fuller, C. J., Holmes, Brewer, and Peckham, JJ., dissented.

(*b*) Condemnation of certain lands under a New York statute for the purpose of an elevated railroad.[4] Injunctions were sought in the State courts by property owners to prevent alleged damages to easements. The contract clause of the Constitution was the predomi-

[1] Roller *v.* Holly, 176 U. S. 398. October Term, 1899.

[2] Kentucky Statutes, Sections 835–839.

[3] Madisonville Traction Co. *v.* Mining Co., 196 U. S. 239. October Term, 1904.

[4] New York Laws, 1892, Chap. 339.

nant issue, although violation of the due process clause of the Fourteenth Amendment was set up. Relief having been denied by the State courts, upon the proper proceedings had, the Supreme Court of the United States upheld the contention of the parties aggrieved.[1] Holmes, J., Fuller, C.J., White and Peckham, JJ., dissented. Brown, J., concurred in the result.

4. *Public health.* A law was passed in the State of New York limiting the working period of employees in bakeries to a maximum of sixty hours per week.[2] Suit was brought to test the constitutionality of this law under the Fourteenth Amendment. The State courts of New York held it to be a valid exercise of the police power. Upon writ of error the Supreme Court of the United States declared the same void on the ground that it operated to violate the liberty of contract under the due process of law clause of the Amendment.[3] Harlan, White, and Day, JJ., dissented. Holmes, J., dissented in a separate opinion.

5. *Conservation of natural resources.* A statute of Oklahoma prohibited the transportation of natural gas from the State and otherwise regulated the transportation of natural gas within the State.[4] A foreign

[1] Muhlker *v.* N. Y. & Harlem R. R. Co., 197 U. S. 544. October Term, 1904.

Birrell *v.* N. Y. & Harlem R. R. Co., 198 U. S. 390. October Term, 1904.

[2] New York Laws, 1897, Chap. 415, Art. 8, Sec. 110.

[3] Lochner *v.* New York, 198 U. S. 45. October Term, 1904.

[4] Oklahoma Laws, 1907, Chap. 67.

gas company secured a Federal injunction restraining the execution of the statute on the ground of violation of the interstate commerce clause of the Constitution and also of deprivation of property without due process of law in contravention of the Fourteenth Amendment. The commerce clause was the predominant issue. On appeal by the State the injunction was sustained.[1] Holmes, Lurton, and Hughes, JJ., dissented.

6. *Anti-trust legislation.* A statute of Illinois for the prevention of monopolies, exempted agricultural products and live stock in the hands of the producer from the operation of the law.[2] On appeal from proceedings in a Federal court, the Supreme Court of the United States declared the act void on the ground that the exemption above mentioned denied the equal protection of the laws in contravention of the Fourteenth Amendment.[3] McKenna, J., dissented.

7. *City problems.* (1) Regulation of the price of gas. The city of Peoria, Illinois, passed an ordinance fixing the maximum price of gas at seventy-five cents per one thousand cubic feet of eighteen candle power.[4] The gas company petitioned for a Federal injunction to restrain the enforcement of the ordinance on the grounds that the rate violated the contract clause of the

[1] Oklahoma *v.* Kansas Natural Gas Co., 221 U. S. 229. October Term, 1910.

[2] Laws of Illinois, 1893, p. 182.

[3] Connolly *v.* Union Sewer Pipe Co., 184 U. S. 540. October Term, 1901.

[4] Peoria Ordinance, September 4, 1900.

Constitution and was confiscatory by virtue of the due process clause of the Fourteenth Amendment. Upon a denial of the petition by the lower court, an appeal was taken to the Supreme Court of the United States, whereupon the lower court was reversed and ordered to grant a temporary injunction pending the taking of testimony.[1] The merits of the case were not decided.

(2) *Prescribing lawful territory for gas-works.* An ordinance of Los Angeles limited the erection of gas-works to certain sections of the city. A later amendment made some changes in the territory prescribed by the original ordinance, thereby excluding from the lawful territory a certain gas plant.[2] Upon proceedings in the State courts, the owner of the gas-works set up the claim that the amendment of the original ordinance deprived him of his property without due process of law in contravention of the Fourteenth Amendment. The State courts upheld the validity of the ordinance. Upon writ of error the Supreme Court of the United States held that the amendment to the ordinance was "an arbitrary and discriminatory exercise of the police power" and therefore void by virtue of the Fourteenth Amendment.[3]

(3) *Public convenience and safety.* The city of San Francisco passsed an ordinance regulating certain phases

[1] Gas Co. *v.* Peoria, 200 U. S. 49. October Term, 1905.

[2] Los Angeles Ordinance, August 26, 1901; amended November 25, 1901.

[3] Dobbins *v.* Los Angeles, 195 U. S. 223. October Term, 1904.

of the laundry business.[1] Certain Chinese set up the claim that the manner in which it was being enforced deprived them of the equal protection of the laws in contravention of the Fourteenth Amendment. Upon certain proceedings had in the State courts and in the lower Federal court, the matter was decided in favor of the city. Upon appellate proceedings in the Supreme Court of the United States, both the State and the Federal courts were reversed and the contention of the Chinese upheld.[2]

(4) *Street improvement.* Two ordinances, one involving an assessment for street paving in Des Moines against the property of a non-resident, and the other a proceeding to condemn certain property for opening a street in the village of Norwood, Ohio, were held by the Supreme Court of the United States to be in violation of the due process clause of the Fourteenth Amendment. The Iowa case was tried in the State courts.[3] In the Ohio case a Federal injunction was allowed, restraining the enforcement of the ordinance.[4] Brewer, Gray, and Shiras, JJ., dissented in the latter case.

(5) *Regulation of street railways.* An ordinance of the city of Cleveland, Ohio, fixed the title to certain rails, poles, and other apparatus owned by the street railway company, in the city, to take effect at the

[1] San Francisco Ordinance, May 26, 1880, and June 28, 1880.
[2] Yick Wo. *v.* Hopkins, 118 U. S. 356. October Term, 1885.
[3] Dewey *v.* Des Moines, 173 U. S. 193. October Term, 1898.
[4] Norwood *v.* Baker, 172 U. S. 269. October Term, 1898.

expiration of the franchise.[1] The company procured a Federal injunction restraining the enforcement of the ordinance on the ground of the violation of the contract clause of the Constitution and, also, of the due process of law clause of the Fourteenth Amendment. Upon appellate proceedings this contention was upheld by the Supreme Court of the United States.[2]

(6) *Regulation of telephone rates.* The enforcement of an ordinance of Memphis, Tennessee, regulating telephone rates,[3] was enjoined by the Federal court upon the petition of the telephone company. A permanent injunction was allowed on the ground that the rates were confiscatory in violation of the due process clause of the Fourteenth Amendment. On appeal by the city the Supreme Court of the United States dismissed the appellate proceedings on the ground that the Federal question under the Amendment did not properly appear from the pleadings.[4] White, C.J., McKenna and Hughes, JJ., dissented.

(7) *Taxation.* (*a*) An ordinance of the city of New Orleans imposing a license tax of $6250 on the American Sugar Refining Company.[5] Proceedings in the State court were removed to the Federal court, on the ground

[1] Cleveland Ordinance, January 11, 1904.

[2] Cleveland Elec. Ry. Co. *v.* Cleveland, 204 U. S. 116. October Term, 1906.

[3] Memphis Ordinance, September 24, 1907.

[4] Memphis *v.* Cumberland Tel. Co., 218 U. S. 624. October Term, 1910.

[5] New Orleans Ordinance, 1898, under Louisiana Act, No. 171, of 1898.

of the non-residence of the company. At the trial the company set up as its defence the violation of the equal protection clause of the Fourteenth Amendment. Verdict having been rendered in favor of the city, the case was taken to the Circuit Court of Appeals on writ of error, where it was dismissed for want of jurisdiction. On further appellate proceedings in the Supreme Court, the Circuit Court of Appeals was reversed, the Court holding that it had jurisdiction of the constitutional question involved, having already jurisdiction by virtue of the non-residence of the company.[1] The merits were not decided.

(*b*) An ordinance of the village of New Hope, Pennsylvania, fixing a license tax of one dollar for each pole and two and one-half dollars for each mile of wire of the telegraph company. The State courts upheld the ordinance. The Supreme Court of the United States, upon writ of error, declared the same void both as a violation of the commerce clause of the Constitution and of the due process clause of the Fourteenth Amendment, the rate being considered unreasonably high.[2] Harlan and Brewer, JJ., dissented.

(*c*) Procedure by the city council of Denver, Colorado, sitting as a board of equalization under the city charter,[3] fixing tax assessments. The defendant in

[1] Am. Sugar Refining Co. *v.* New Orleans, 181 U. S. 277. October Term, 1900.

[2] Postal-Tel. Cable Co. *v.* New Hope, 192 U. S. 55. October Term, 1903.

[3] Denver Charter, 1893, Art. 7, Sec. 3, 29–31.

this case claimed that the assessment was void by virtue of the due process clause of the Fourteenth Amendment in that he was given no opportunity to be heard. Having been denied relief by the State courts, upon writ of error the Supreme Court of the United States upheld his contention.[1] Fuller, C.J., and Holmes, J., dissented.

8. *The negro race question.* There have been six instances of Federal intervention under the Amendment on this point;[2] four growing out of ante-bellum or reconstruction laws and procedure, and two others — one in 1899 and the other in 1903. Each involve the single question of excluding negroes from the jury service. In none of them were the merits of the alleged discrimination decided by the Supreme Court of the United States. In four of these cases there were dissenting opinions.[3]

9. *State taxation.* (1) Validity of assessment. (*a*) Procedure under the laws of Georgia [4] to collect back taxes from a railroad. The company set up the claim in the State courts that the enforcement of this law deprived it of its property without due process of law,

[1] Londoner *v.* Denver, 210 U. S. 373. October Term, 1907.

[2] Strauder *v.* West Virginia, 100 U. S. 303. October Term, 1879.

Ex parte Virginia, 100 U. S. 339. October Term, 1879.
Neal *v.* Delaware, 103 U. S. 370. October Term, 1880.
Bush *v.* Kentucky, 107 U. S. 110. October Term, 1882.
Carter *v.* Texas, 177 U. S. 442. October Term, 1899.
Rogers *v.* Alabama, 192 U. S. 226. October Term, 1903.

[3] See *ante*, Chaps. V and VI.

[4] Georgia Political Code, Secs. 804–805, 812–814, 847, 855, 874, 879.

as provided by the Fourteenth Amendment. The State courts decided in favor of the validity of the statute. Upon writ of error the Supreme Court of the United States sustained the contention of the railroad company.[1]

(b) *Assessment by the Cook County Board of Equalization under the laws of Illinois.*[2] The Chicago Traction Company and six other corporations, upon petition in the Federal court, secured an injunction restraining the collection of taxes under the above assessment on the ground that the rates were discriminatory, thereby depriving them of the equal protection of the laws. On appeal by the county, the Supreme Court of the United States sustained the injunction.[3] Holmes and Moody, JJ., dissented.

(2) *Taxation of personal property when the situs is in another State.* (a) *Pennsylvania.* Taxation of coal in West Virginia owned by a Pennsylvania railroad.[4] Upon proper proceedings the State courts were reversed by the Supreme Court of the United States and the assessment held void as a violation of the due process clause of the Fourteenth Amendment.[5] Fuller, C.J., dissented.

[1] Cent. Ga. Ry. Co. *v.* Wright, Compr., 207 U. S. 127. October Term, 1907.

[2] Const. Ill., 1870, Art. 9, Sec. 1, and Hurd's Revised Statutes, 1899.

[3] Raymond, Treas. *v.* Chicago Trac. Co., 207 U. S. 20. October Term, 1907.

[4] Pennsylvania Laws, 1891, p. 229.

[5] Del., L. & W. R. R. Co. *v.* Pennsylvania, 198 U. S. 341. October Term, 1904.

(*b*) *Kentucky*. Taxation of cars in Indiana owned by a Kentucky railroad under a statute subjecting the personal property of all citizens of Kentucky to taxation in that State regardless of the *situs*.[1] The law was declared valid by the State courts. Upon appellate proceedings in the Supreme Court of the United States it was pronounced void in that it took property without due process of law and denied the equal protection of the laws, in violation of the Fourteenth Amendment.[2] Holmes, J., and Fuller, C.J., dissented.

Kentucky. Taxation of a franchise in Indiana.[3] The proceedings were similar to the above, the tax being held void under the due process clause of the Amendment.[4] Fuller, C.J., and Shiras, J., dissented.

Kentucky. Taxation of whiskey stored in Germany by owners in Kentucky who held the warehouse receipts. The tax was declared void under the due process clause of the Amendment under procedure similar to the above.[5]

(3) *Taxation of personal property when the owner thereof is a non-resident of the State.* (*a*) *Indiana*. Taxation of notes owned in New York and payable in Ohio.

[1] Sec. 4020, Kentucky Statutes.

[2] Union Transit Co. *v.* Kentucky, 199 U. S. 194. October Term, 1905.

[3] Sec. 4077 *et seq.*, Kentucky Revised Statutes.

[4] Louisville, etc., Ferry Co. *v.* Kentucky, 188 U. S. 385. October Term, 1902.

[5] Selliger *v.* Kentucky, 213 U. S. 200. October Term, 1908.

The amount involved was \$750,000. The Indiana assessment was \$36,357.71. The notes were sent to Indiana presumably to escape taxation in Ohio. Proceedings in the State courts resulted in a verdict for the State. Upon writ of error the Supreme Court of the United States declared the tax void in that it was a taking of property without due process of law in violation of the Fourteenth Amendment.[1] Day and Brewer, JJ., dissented.

(*b*) *Louisiana*. Taxation of credit notes and bank deposits held in New Orleans by a corporation of New York.[2] The amount involved was \$636,900. An injunction from the Federal court restraining the collection of the tax was sustained on appeal, by the Supreme Court of the United States under the due process clause of the Amendment as in the above case.[3] Brewer, J., dissented.

(4) *Franchise taxes on corporations*. (*a*) *California*. Upon suit by the State the company petitioned for a removal of the cause to the Federal court under Act of Congress, March 3, 1875, as a suit arising under the Constitution of the United States, violation of the due process and the equal protection clauses of the Fourteenth Amendment being alleged. Upon a denial of the petition by the State courts and proper proceedings

[1] Buck *v*. Beach, 206 U. S. 392. October Term, 1906.

[2] Louisiana Acts, 1898, No. 170.

[3] New Orleans *v*. New York Life Ins. Co., 216 U. S. 517. October Term, 1909.

had, the Supreme Court of the United States decided in favor of the petitioner.[1]

(*b*) *Kansas*. A statute fixing a charter fee for corporations based on a certain per cent of the entire capital stock, the same to be paid into the school fund of the State.[2] In this case the fee was $20,100. After proceedings in the State courts in which the law was held valid, the Supreme Court of the United States, upon writ of error, declared the statute void in that (1) it imposed a burden on interstate commerce, and (2) it violated the due process and the equal protection clauses of the Fourteenth Amendment in taxing property beyond the limits of the State. The defendant was a foreign corporation. The commerce clause was the predominant issue.[3] Fuller, C.J., Holmes, McKenna, and Peckham, JJ., dissented.

Kansas. The same statute brought in question in *quo warranto* proceedings against the Pullman Company with the same result as in the above.[4] Fuller, C.J., Holmes, and McKenna, JJ., dissented.

(*c*) *Arkansas*. A statute known as the Wingo Act fixed the charter fee of foreign corporations on the same basis as the Kansas law above mentioned.[5] The char-

[1] Sou. Pac. R. R. Co. *v*. California, 118 U. S. 109. October Term, 1885. [2] Kansas General Statute, 1901, p. 280.

[3] West. Union Tel. Co. *v*. Kansas, 216 U. S., 1. October Term, 1909.

[4] Pullman Co. *v*. Kansas, 216 U. S. 156. October Term, 1909.

[5] Arkansas Laws, 1907, p. 744.

ter fee in this case was $25,050. A Federal injunction restraining the enforcement of the statute was sustained on appeal by the State, on the authority of the opinions in the Kansas cases.[1] Fuller, C.J., Holmes, and McKenna, JJ., dissented.

(*d*) *Alabama.* A statute classifying corporations into foreign and domestic and fixing a charter fee for foreign corporations at a certain per cent of the entire capital stock in use within the borders of the State.[2] After proceedings in the State courts in which the statute was upheld, the Supreme Court of the United States declared it void in that it deprived the foreign corporations, doing business within the State, of the equal protection of the laws, in contravention of the Fourteenth Amendment.[3] Fuller, C.J., Holmes, and McKenna, JJ., dissented.

10. *State regulation of public service corporations.* (1) Stock-yards. *Kansas.* A statute regulating public stock-yards, fixing charges, prescribing duties, and fixing penalties.[4] A Federal injunction restraining the enforcement of the statute was sustained by the Supreme

[1] Ludwig *v.* West. Union Tel. Co., 216 U. S. 146. October Term, 1909.

[2] Alabama Code, 1907, Vol. I, p. 986, Secs. 2391–2400.

[3] Sou. Ry. Co. *v.* Greene, 216 U. S. 400. October Term, 1909.

L. & N. R. R. Co. *v.* Gaston, 216 U. S. 418. October Term, 1909.

Cent. Ga. R. R. Co. *v.* Gaston, 216 U. S. 418. October Term, 1909.

[4] Kansas Laws, March 3, 1897.

Court of the United States, on appeal by the State, on the ground that the statute operated only against the Kansas City Stock-Yards Company, thereby violating the equal protection clause of the Fourteenth Amendment.[1]

(2) *Insurance companies.* (*a*) *Louisiana.* A statute prohibiting the dealing with foreign insurance companies which had not complied with the laws of Louisiana.[2] The law was declared valid by the State courts. Upon writ of error the Supreme Court of the United States held that it violated the due process clause of the Amendment in that it worked a deprivation of the liberty of contract.[3]

(*b*) *Indiana. Pennsylvania.* A judgment was rendered in a Pennsylvania State court against an insurance company under a statute providing that service of process on the insurance commissioner was sufficient notice.[4] "Full faith and credit" was given this judgment in the Indiana courts. Upon writ of error the Supreme Court of the United States declared both judgments void in that the service on the insurance commissioner was insufficient, thereby violating the due process clause of the Fourteenth Amendment.[5]

[1] Cotting *v.* Kansas City Stock-Yards Co., 183 U. S. 79. October Term, 1901.

[2] Louisiana Laws, 1894, No. 66.

[3] Allgeyer *v.* Louisiana, 165 U. S., 578. October Term, 1896.

[4] Pennsylvania Laws, June 20, 1883.

[5] Old Wayne Life Ins. Assn. *v.* McDonough, 204 U. S. 8. October Term, 1906.

(3) *Recovery of land from railroads. Texas.* A suit in 1890 to recover certain sections of land from a railroad company under a legislative grant in 1866 on the ground that the grant was made without authority.[1] Judgment having been rendered for the State in the State courts, upon proceedings in the Supreme Court of the United States, the State courts were reversed under the contract clause of the Constitution and under the due process clause of the Fourteenth Amendment. The contract clause was the predominant issue.[2]

(4) *Regulation of the collection of claims against railroads. Texas.* A statute allowing a ten-dollar attorney's fee as a part of the judgment for the plaintiff on certain claims against railroads under certain conditions.[3] After being upheld in the courts of the State, the statute was declared void by the Supreme Court of the United States in that it violated the due process and the equal protection clauses of the Fourteenth Amendment.[4] Gray, J., Fuller, C.J., and White, J., dissented.

(5) *Regulation of railroad profits. Indiana.* A statute regulating the profits of railroads within the State.[5] In this case the construction of a charter of

[1] Constitution of Texas, 1869, Sec. 6, Art. 10.

[2] Houston & Tex. Cent. Ry. Co. *v.* Texas, 170 U. S. 243. October Term, 1897.

[3] Sayles, *Supp. Tex. Civil Stat.*, p. 768, Art. 4266a.

[4] Gulf, Colo. & Santa Fe Ry. *v.* Ellis, 165 U. S. 150. October Term, 1896.

[5] Indiana Laws, January 27, February 24, and March 4, 1897.

1847 was involved. Upon proceedings by writ of error the Supreme Court of the United States declared the law violative of the contract clause of the Constitution and of the due process clause of the Fourteenth Amendment. The contract clause was the predominant issue.[1]

(6) *Compulsory improvement of the railroad service.* (*a*) *Nebraska.* An order of the State Board of Transportation compelling a railroad company to allow the erection of certain grain elevators on its right of way.[2] A mandamus was awarded by the State court to enforce this order. Upon writ of error the Supreme Court of the United States declared the proceedings to be in violation of the due process clause of the Fourteenth Amendment.[3]

(*b*) *Nebraska.* A statute compelling railroad companies to construct and maintain certain side-tracks and switches for certain grain elevators adjacent to the right of way.[4] After procedure in the State courts upholding the statute, the Supreme Court of the United States declared it unconstitutional on the grounds mentioned in the preceding case.[5] Harlan and McKenna, JJ., dissented.

[1] T. H. & Ind. R. R. Co. *v.* Indiana, 194 U. S. 579. October Term, 1903.

[2] December 13, 1889.

[3] Mo. Pac. Ry. *v.* Nebraska, 164 U. S. 403. October Term, 1896.

[4] Nebraska Session Laws, 1905, Chap. 105, Secs. 1, 6.

[5] Mo. Pac. Ry. Co. *v.* Nebraska, 217 U. S. 196. October Term, 1909.

(*c*) *Kentucky*. A provision of the State Constitution compelling railroad companies, under certain conditions, to deliver cars to other railroads.[1] After procedure in the State courts upholding the constitutional provision, the Supreme Court of the United States declared it void in that it placed a burden on interstate commerce and violated the due process clause of the Fourteenth Amendment.[2] McKenna, Harlan, and Moody, JJ., dissented.

(7) *Regulation of the rates of common carriers.* (*a*) *Texas*. Fixing the rates by the Railroad Commission.[3] A Federal injunction was sustained by the Supreme Court of the United States, on appeal by the State, on the ground that the proposed rates worked a deprivation of property without due process of law and denied the equal protection of the laws, in violation of the Fourteenth Amendment. The Eleventh Amendment was also involved.[4]

(*b*) *Minnesota*. 1887. An order of the Railroad and Warehouse Commission fixing rates.[5] A mandamus was awarded by the State courts to compel compliance with the order. Upon writ of error the Supreme Court

[1] Kentucky Constitution, Secs. 213–214.

[2] L. & N. R. R. Co. *v*. Cent. Stock-Yards Co., 212 U. S. 132. October Term, 1908.

[3] Texas Laws, April 3, 1891.

[4] Reagan *v*. Farmers' Loan & Trust Co., 154 U. S. 362. October Term, 1893.

Reagan *v*. Mercantile Trust Co., 154 U. S. 413. October Term, 1893.

[5] Minnesota Gen. Laws, Chap. 10, 1887.

of the United States annulled the order on the ground that it violated the due process and the equal protection clauses of the Fourteenth Amendment, in that the notice of the hearing was insufficient.[1] Bradley, Gray, and Lamar, JJ., dissented.

(c) *Minnesota.* 1907. Certain statutes provided for a two-cent passenger rate and the regulation of freight rates.[2] Penalties were also fixed. A Federal injunction was allowed, restraining the attorney-general of the State from enforcing the statute on the ground that such enforcement would work a deprivation of property without due process of law contrary to the Fourteenth Amendment. The attorney-general refused to obey the injunction and was thereupon confined for contempt. He petitioned for a writ of *habeas corpus* in the Supreme Court of the United States on the ground that the injunction was in violation of the Eleventh Amendment. His petition was denied. The merits of the rate law were not decided.[3] Harlan, J., dissented.

(d) *Kentucky.* A statute reducing tolls.[4] An injunction was granted by the State courts to prevent a contravention of the statute. Upon writ of error the Supreme Court of the United States dissolved the injunction on the ground that the statute was a *prima facie* violation of the due process and the equal pro-

[1] Chicago, Mil. & St. P. Ry. *v.* Minnesota, 134 U. S. 418. October Term, 1889. [2] Minnesota Rate Laws, 1905, 1906, 1907.

[3] *Ex parte* Young, 209 U. S. 125. October Term, 1907.

[4] Kentucky Laws, 1890.

tection clauses of the Fourteenth Amendment. The merits were not decided.[1]

(*e*) *Kentucky*. An order of the Railroad Commission fixing general tariff rates.[2] A Federal injunction preventing the enforcement of the order was sustained by the Supreme Court of the United States, on appeal by the State, under the due process and equal protection clauses of the Fourteenth Amendment on the ground that the commission exceeded its authority. The commerce clause was also involved.[3]

(*f*) *Nebraska*. An order of the Board of Transportation fixing freight rates.[4] A Federal injunction restraining the enforcement of the order was sustained by the Supreme Court of the United States, on appeal by the State, under the due process and equal protection clauses of the Fourteenth Amendment on the ground that the rates were too low.[5]

(*g*) *Nebraska*. This was a further attempt to enforce the above-mentioned rate law. A Federal injunction was sustained as in the above.[6]

(*h*) *South Dakota*. Order of the Railroad Commission regulating rates.[7] A petition for an injunction

[1] Covington Turnpike Co. *v*. Sanford, 164 U. S. 578. October Term, 1896.

[2] Kentucky Laws, March 10, 1900.

[3] Silver *v*. L. & N. R. R. Co., 213 U. S. 175. October Term, 1908.

[4] Nebraska Rate Law, April 12, 1893.

[5] Smyth *v*. Ames, 169 U. S. 466. October Term, 1897.

[6] Prout *v*. Starr, 188 U. S. 537. October Term, 1902.

[7] South Dakota Laws, 1897, Chap. 110.

on the basis of a violation of the Fourteenth Amendment was denied by the Federal court. On appeal the Supreme Court of the United States granted a temporary injunction with instructions to refer the case to a master to ascertain the facts.[1]

(*i*) *Michigan.* A statute of Michigan provided, among other things, that 1000-mile railroad tickets should be valid for two years from the date of purchase and redeemable within that time at the rate of three cents per mile.[2] After procedure in the State courts in which the provision was declared valid, the Supreme Court of the United States, upon writ of error, held it to be void under the due process and the equal protection clauses of the Fourteenth Amendment.[3] Fuller, C.J., Gray, and McKenna, JJ., dissented.

The foregoing bare outline of facts is shown here void of local coloring. The peculiar circumstances which gave rise to the laws in question, the reasons which led the State courts to uphold them, and the public opinion of the States which approved them cannot be shown in this study, nor can they be fully understood by those living outside of the State in question, unconnected with the local problem involved. In such a presentation as this we see only one side of the question — the Federal side.

[1] Chicago, Mil. & St. P. Ry. *v.* Tompkins, 176 U. S. 167. October Term, 1899.

[2] Michigan Laws, 1891, Act No. 90, Sec. 9.

[3] Lake Shore & Mich. Ry. *v.* Smith, 173 U. S. 684. October Term, 1898.

Chart No. III

TERRITORIAL OPERATION OF FEDERAL INTERVENTION UNDER THE FOURTEENTH AMENDMENT, 1868–1911

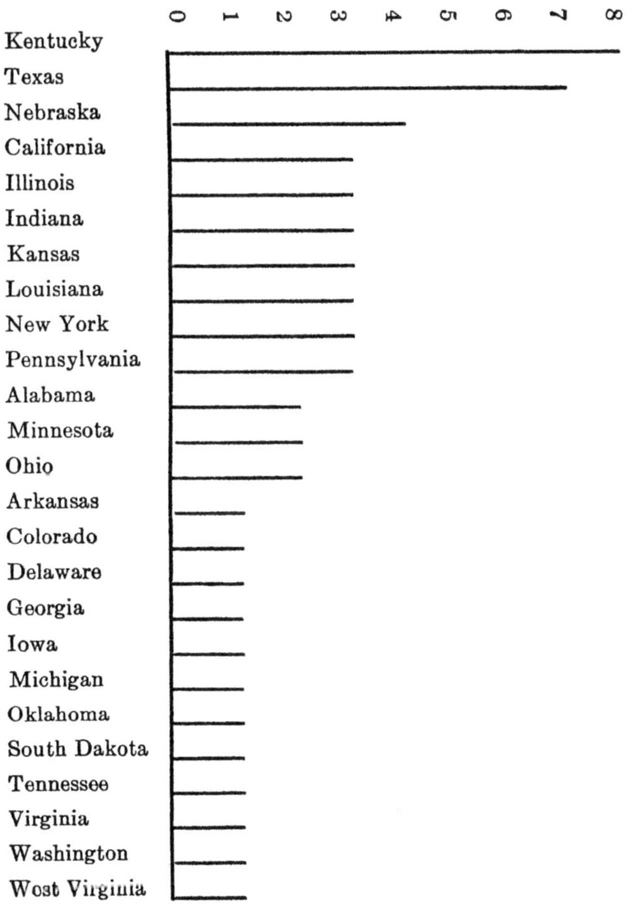

Within the past forty-three years twenty-five States have been directly affected by Federal intervention under the Amendment. This involved the annulment in whole or in part of thirty-two statutes, nine city ordinances, and a portion of four State constitutions. As to the total number of the fifty-five instances of intervention, eleven were made under the equal protection clause of the Amendment, six of these involving the right of negroes to sit on juries; fourteen were made under the equal protection and the due process of law clauses considered together; and the remaining thirty were made under the due process of law clause alone, two as deprivations of liberty without due process of law, and twenty-eight as taking property without due process of law.

Although there are before us six hundred and four opinions handed down by the Supreme Court of the United States under the Fourteenth Amendment, in fifty-five of which the Federal Government was allowed to intervene in the affairs of the State, it is very difficult to formulate general principles governing this intervention. The terms "due process of law" and "equal protection of the laws," for this purpose, mean nothing in themselves. They gain their meaning only from the conditions and circumstances of each particular case. Matters of time, space, and manner govern their interpretation. They cannot be detached from the concrete local environment.

However, we can trace the path in which Federal

intervention has heretofore moved and see something of its chronological development. The first instance of intervention was in 1879, eleven years after the adoption of the Amendment, when a law of the State of West Virginia was declared void because it excluded negroes from the jury service.[1] In 1885 the enforcement of an ordinance in California was restrained on account of discrimination against the Chinese.[2] In 1889 the State of Minnesota was restrained from enforcing its railroad rate law.[3] This was followed by similar action as to the Texas rate law of 1893,[4] and the Nebraska rate law in 1897.[5]

In 1896 the State of Nebraska was prohibited from enforcing a law regulating the erection of grain elevators on the right of way of railroads,[6] and the State of Louisiana from enforcing a law regulating the dealing of its citizens with foreign insurance companies.[7] In 1898 the enforcement of one city ordinance in Ohio,[8] and another in Iowa,[9] was restrained as taking property without due process of law. In 1901 a stock-yard law of Kansas [10] and an anti-trust law of Illinois [11] were

[1] Strauder *v.* West Virginia, 100 U. S. 303.
[2] Yick Wo *v.* Hopkins, 118 U. S. 356.
[3] Chicago, Mil. & St. P. Ry. *v.* Minnesota, 134 U. S. 418.
[4] Reagan *v.* Farmers' Loan & Trust Co., 154 U. S. 362.
[5] Smyth *v.* Ames, 169 U. S. 466.
[6] Mo. Pac. Ry. *v.* Nebraska, 164 U. S. 403.
[7] Allgeyer *v.* Louisiana, 165 U. S. 578.
[8] Norwood *v.* Baker, 172 U. S. 269.
[9] Dewey *v.* Des Moines, 173 U. S. 193.
[10] Cotting *v.* Kansas, 183 U. S. 79.
[11] Connolly *v.* Union Sewer Pipe Co., 184 U. S. 540.

annulled. In 1904 a law of New York regulating the hours of labor in bakeries was declared void.[1] In 1907 the States of Georgia and Illinois were restrained from collecting certain taxes from certain corporations.[2] In 1909 the enforcement of the franchise tax laws of Arkansas,[3] Kansas,[4] and Alabama,[5] and a law of Nebraska regulating railroad side-tracks and switches,[6] were restrained.

We thus see that Federal intervention under the Amendment has gradually drifted away from race questions and has within recent years entered other fields of State activity. It has become directly related to the most serious problems that engage the nation. This gradual development of intervention under the Amendment has not been accomplished without opposition, even in the Supreme Court of the United States itself. In ten of the eighteen cases above cited there were dissenting opinions.

We cannot answer the question as to how far Federal intervention can go under the Fourteenth Amendment. We can see how far it has gone, but a study of all of these cases fails to enable one to set limitations for the Amendment in the future, under the present Federal

[1] Lochner *v.* New York, 198 U. S. 45.

[2] Central of Ga. Ry. Co. *v.* Wright, 207 U. S. 127.
Raymond, Treas. Cook Co. *v.* Chicago Trac. Co., 207 U. S. 20.

[3] Ludwig *v.* West. Union Tel. Co., 216 U. S. 146.

[4] West. Union Tel. Co. *v.* Kansas, 216 U. S. 1.
Pullman Co. *v.* Kansas, 216 U. S. 156.

[5] Sou. Ry. Co. *v.* Greene, 216 U. S. 400.

[6] Mo. Pac. Ry. Co. *v.* Nebraska, 217 U. S. 196.

procedure. For practical purposes this principle of intervention may be stated in the following words: No State can make or enforce any laws which shall, upon proper proceedings, be deemed unreasonable by a majority of the Supreme Court of the United States. This involves the interpretation in each case of the terms "due process of law" and "equal protection of the laws." The rule of reason alone governs. What are fair profits, what are excessive taxes, what are proper health laws, what is confiscation and what discrimination, — these are questions which cannot be answered in the abstract, nor can they be adequately defined by precedents. If it becomes incumbent on the Supreme Court of the United States to pass judgment on them, it must consider the reasonableness of each concrete case.

CHAPTER VIII

Stare Decisis

The principle voiced in the maxim, *stare decisis et non quieta movere* — to stand by precedents and not to disturb what is settled—has been known to all systems of judicature. Former judicial decisions as a source of law were recognized as far back as the ancient Egyptians. In some measure this principle operated in the Roman law and is not without force in those modern outgrowths of the Roman system.[1]

The full development of this doctrine is found in the English Common Law. It is founded on the principle that stability and certainty in the law are of first importance. When a point of law is once clearly decided by a court of final jurisdiction, it becomes a fixed rule of law to govern future action. The certainty of the law is regarded as of more importance than the reason of it. It is better to have a bad law with certainty of its meaning than a good law whose scope of operation is indefinable and unknown.

The doctrine of *stare decisis* is of the utmost importance to the whole Anglo-American system of judica-

[1] See *Harvard Law Review*, Vol. IX, p. 31: *Judicial Precedents*, by John Chipman Gray.

ture. The case system of the study and the practice of law is based directly upon it. It operates strongest where rights of contract or property *inter partes* are involved. The reason is apparent. When property rights are once fixed, especially titles to real property, they cannot be disturbed without great injustice to those who have based their actions and entered into business relations on the basis of such former decision. Faith in the stability of the law is essential to the health of the business world. *Misera est servitus ubi jus vagum aut incertum.* The courts are not at liberty to consider cases *de novo.*

On the other hand, the doctrine of *stare decisis* is much weaker in the realm of constitutional law. This is inevitable. Constitutional law is organic. It grows. It is an expression of the life of the social organism. This phase of the public law cannot be bound by precedents to the same extent as private law.

The principle of *stare decisis* is of peculiar importance in its relation to the operation of the Fourteenth Amendment to the Constitution of the United States. We shall confine our study to section one of that article, the other four sections being now possessed of little or no vitality. It reads as follows: "All persons born or naturalized in the United States, and subject to the jurisdiction thereof, are citizens of the United States and of the States wherein they reside. No State shall make or enforce any law which shall abridge the privileges or immunities of citizens of the United

States; nor shall any State deprive any person of life, liberty, or property without due process of law; nor deny to any person within its jurisdiction the equal protection of the laws."

Now this section does not define itself. Its terminology, although time-honored among people of English stock, is, in its new setting, vague, indefinite, and uncertain. Under our constitutional system the Supreme Court of the United States is the only organ of the government to which the people can look for a definition. Cases under the Amendment began coming before that tribunal as early as 1873, but the Court thought it wiser to leave the definition of the scope and the meaning of its terms to the operation of the doctrine of *stare decisis* rather than to attempt a definition of the whole provision outright. Thus by the gradual process of judicial inclusion and exclusion it was intended that there should be accumulated in the course of time a long line of judicial precedents based on concrete cases presented for decision, which would in themselves define the terms of the Amendment.[1]

In adopting this course, the Court followed its usual custom of considering only those points which were properly presented and vital to the issue. In this particular, the operation of the doctrine of *stare decisis* is reduced to a minimum, quantitatively, because if a case can be disposed of on a lesser point, the greater

[1] Cf. Davidson *v.* New Orleans, 96 U. S. 97, and Holden *v.* Hardy, 169 U. S. 366.

will not be considered. The following extract from the opinion in the Slaughter House Cases [1] is an illustration in point: "Having shown that the privileges and immunities relied on in the argument are those which belong to the citizens of the State as such, and that they are left to the State governments for security and protection, and not by this article placed under the special care of the Federal Government, we may hold ourselves excused from defining the privileges and immunities of citizens of the United States which no State can abridge, until some case involving those privileges may make it necessary to do so." The Court in this case defined neither citizenship in the United States nor citizenship in the States, but declared in effect that in the particular case before it the Federal Government could under the Fourteenth Amendment give no relief from State activity.

From the adoption of the Amendment in 1868 to the close of the 1910–1911 Term of the Supreme Court, six hundred and four opinions have been delivered under section one of that article. We have now a line of decisions running back for forty-one years. Has the operation of the doctrine of *stare decisis* effected a definition of the Amendment? Is its sphere of operation now known? These questions must be answered in the negative. After forty years from the date of the adoption of the Amendment, Mr. Justice Moody, in delivering the opinion of the Court in a recent

[1] 16 Wall. 78.

case, could say: "The Fourteenth Amendment withdrew from the States powers theretofore enjoyed by them, to an extent not yet fully ascertained."[1] In a still more recent case, after five hundred and sixty-seven cases involving an interpretation of the "due process of law" clause under the Amendment had been considered by the Court, Mr. Justice Holmes, in delivering the opinion, said, "What is due process of law depends on the circumstances."[2]

We have made but little progress in reaching even a working definition of section one of the Fourteenth Amendment under the operation of the principle of *stare decisis*. This would be a matter of small practical concern were it not for the fact that the Amendment is fruitful of more litigation before the courts of the country to-day than is any other provision of the Constitution. It is becoming more and more intertwined with the great economic questions of the day. An increasing amount of the time and energy of the Supreme Court of the United States is being consumed in disposing of questions arising under it.

What is "due process of law"; what is "equal protection"; what are the "privileges or immunities of citizens of the United States"; what the relations between citizenship in the United States and State citizenship — we do not exactly know. The policy of the Supreme Court is to wait until a sufficient number

[1] Twining *v.* New Jersey, 211 U. S. 92 (1908).
[2] Moyer *v.* Peabody, 212 U. S. 84 (1909).

of cases have arisen that they themselves will define every phase of the Amendment. This is the only logical position for the Court to take. The difficulty is unavoidable. It is practically impossible to define the Amendment outright, and any attempt to do so would be without precedent and dangerous.

The fault is not with the Court, but is inherent in the Amendment itself. Its terms are elastic, vague, and indefinite. They are so general and so comprehensive as to embrace within the scope of their operation the entire range of the civil rights of the individual. It is capable of more adaptation, more expansion, and more extension than is any other portion of the Federal Constitution, not even excepting the commerce clause. Its place in American constitutional law is historically and logically anomalous.

Under the operation of the principle of *stare decisis*, even under more favorable circumstances than now exist, it would require hundreds of years and thousands of cases before anything like an adequate definition could be gleaned bit by bit from the long line of precedents. This means that the essential elements of the Amendment will never be defined. It will always remain a vague, indefinite, and uncertain measure. The circumstances surrounding our social life are constantly changing. The political ideals of one generation are superseded by those of the next; and since the Fourteenth Amendment attempts to deal with the most vital problem in our governmental system

— the relations of the States to the Federal Government — we may not hope for a definition of its terms from the operation of the principle of *stare decisis.*

This situation is unfortunate. It is very important that the States should know where they stand in the Federal Government. This is especially true in matters economic, where property rights are involved. Within the past forty years the Supreme Court has delivered more than four hundred opinions involving the one question of the States taking property without due process of law. Less than one hundred of these cases arose prior to 1896. More than one-half of all of them deal with the relations of the States to the corporations — the public service companies forming the predominating element. This is, therefore, an intensely modern question and one, it seems, which cannot be solved by the courts.

The actual operation of the principle of *stare decisis* in the judicial history of the Amendment is as complex as it is interesting. A case is "followed," "affirmed," "reaffirmed," "applied," "approved," "considered," "explained," "reconciled," "distinguished," "qualified," or "reversed." Each of these words has in this connection become a quasi-technical term. Each is a shade different from the other in meaning in the order named. Each has its own proper function in designating the attitude which the Court assumes toward the former decision under consideration. Now the Court seldom comes out boldly and reverses itself. Such a procedure would indeed appear unseemly. It is necessary for the sake of stability and propriety that the Supreme Court of the United States maintain an apparent infallibility. But since the laws of evolution do not spare even this high tribunal, and since here also there must be adaptation, discovery, and change to correspond to the growing life of a progressive people, reversals of previous opinions sometimes become necessary. The Supreme Court, bulwark of stability that it is in our constitutional system, in interpreting the Supreme Law of the Land, must ultimately yield to the persistent force of public opinion. The changed attitude of the court is usually expressed by "explaining," "distinguishing," "qualifying," etc., the prior opinion in question. For example, twenty-three cases were "distinguished" at the 1910–1911 Term of the Court. The effect is often a reversal in whole or in part, resulting in a partial or complete change of front. The method is in keeping with the learning and the dignity of that august body, but it involves a species of mental gymnastics that strikes the uninitiated with admiration and amazement.[1]

Now the application of these principles to the in-

[1] The following may be used as an illustration: In *Ex parte* Harding, 219 U. S. 365 (February, 1911), Mr. Chief Justice White, in delivering the opinion, said, "We must then either reconcile the cases, or, if this cannot be done, determine which line rests upon the right principle, and having so determined, overrule or qualify the others and apply and enforce the correct doctrine." In this particular case *Ex parte* Howard, 105 U. S. 578, and the cases following it were applied; Virginia *v.* Rives, 100 U. S. 313, and cases

terpretation of the Fourteenth Amendment produces considerable uncertainty and confusion. As has been said before, the difficulty is inherent. Not many months ago, Mr, Justice Holmes in a dissenting opinion in an important case under the Amendment, made the following remarks: "I think the tax in question was lawful under all the decisions of this court until last week. I have not heard and have not been able to frame any reason that I honestly can say seems to me to justify the judgment of the court in point of law."[1] A few days before, when the same question was decided in West. Union Tel. Co. *v.* Kansas, 216 U. S. 55, Mr. Justice Holmes, dissenting, said: "It appears to me ground for regret that the court so soon should abandon its latest decision."

This is a clear illustration of the point under consideration. Did the court here reverse itself? Mr. Justice Holmes thought so, and with him agreed Mr. Justice McKenna and Mr. Chief Justice Fuller. But the majority of the court declared no such intention. In fact, it was following the doctrine of *stare decisis.* In other words, under a constitutional provision so phrased as is the Fourteenth Amendment, the lines of legal distinctions can be so finely drawn that even the

following it, distinguished; and *Ex parte* Wisner, 203 U. S. 449, *In re* Moore, 209 U. S. 490, and *In re* Winn, 213 U. S. 458 disapproved in part and qualified.

[1] Pullman Co. *v.* Kansas, 216 U. S. 77. The prior decision in question was Security Mutual Life Ins. Co. *v.* Prewitt, 202 U. S. 246.

most experienced jurists cannot agree on the relationship of one case to the other in the line of precedents.

In every branch of the law the rule of *stare decisis* is subject to occasional exceptions. These changes of position by the courts are extremely rare in questions dealing with the law of contracts and of property. The law here remains practically certain from generation to generation. But in the line of decisions under the Fourteenth Amendment uncertainty has been the rule. The Supreme Court has never been able to make here a practical application of the doctrine of *stare decisis*. Dissenting opinions have been prevalent all along the line. The first case under the Amendment was decided by a divided court of four against five.[1] Prior to 1883 there were twenty-five cases before the Court under the Amendment. Ten of these, including practically every important case, were accompanied by dissenting opinions. In the lengthy and learned dissent of Mr. Justice Harlan in the Civil Rights Cases,[2] the following language is found: "The opinion in these cases proceeds, it seems to me, upon grounds entirely too narrow and artificial. I cannot resist the conclusion that the substance and spirit of the recent Amendments of the Constitution have been sacrificed by a subtle and ingenious verbal criticism." This is an extreme illustration of how the Court is often divided in the matter of interpreting the Amendment.

[1] The Slaughter House Cases, 16 Wal. 36.
[2] 109 U. S. 26.

From 1872 to the close of the 1910–1911 Term of the Court, out of six hundred and four opinions delivered, one hundred and fifty-five were accompanied by dissenting opinions. This includes nearly all of the cases of real importance. The relation of this situation to the doctrine of *stare decisis* can readily be seen. While all of these cases are final in so far as they relate to the immediate parties, from the standpoint of judicial precedents as a source of law they are of questionable value.

Let us take one more concrete illustration. On November 3, 1896, there was submitted to the Supreme Court a case involving the constitutionality of the following Texas statute, under the Fourteenth Amendment:[1]—

"SECTION 1. *Be it enacted by the legislature of the State of Texas,* That after the time when this act shall take effect, any person in this State having a *bona fide* claim for personal services rendered or labor done, or for damages, or for overcharges on freight, or claims for stock killed or injured by the train of any railway company, provided that such claims for stock killed or injured shall be presented to the agent of the company nearest the point where such stock was killed or injured, against any railway corporation operating a railroad in this State, and the amount of such claim does not exceed $50, may present the same verified by his affidavit, for payment to such corporation by filing it with any station agent of such corporation in any county where suit may be instituted for the same, and if, at the expiration of thirty days after such pres-

[1] Gulf, Colo., & Santa Fe Ry. *v.* Ellis, 165 U. S. 150.

entation, such claim has not been paid or satisfied, he may immediately institute suit thereon in the proper court; and if he shall finally establish his claim, and obtain judgment for the full amount thereof, as presented for payment to such corporation in such court or any court to which the suit may have been appealed, he shall be entitled to recover the amount of such claim and all costs of suit, and in addition thereto all reasonable attorney's fees, provided he has an attorney employed in his case, not to exceed $10, to be assessed and awarded by the court or jury trying the issue." [1]

Let us call this the Ellis Case. The only point in controversy was the constitutionality of the clause relating to the attorney's fees. The statute had been upheld by the District Court, by the Court of Civil Appeals, and by the Supreme Court of Texas, respectively.[2] The majority of the Supreme Court of the United States declared the statute null and void by reason of the Fourteenth Amendment in that the provision relating to the attorney's fees permitted the taking of property "without due process of law" and denied to the railroad companies the "equal protection of the laws." The opinion was delivered by Mr. Justice Brewer, with whom concurred Justices Field, Harlan, Brown, Shiras, and Peckham. Forty-two cases were cited as precedents in the opinion of the court. A dissenting opinion was delivered by Mr. Justice Gray, upholding the constitutionality of the statute, with whom concurred Mr. Justice White and Mr.

[1] Sayles, *Supplement to Texas Civil Statutes*, p. 768, Art. 4266a.

[2] 87 Texas 19.

Chief Justice Fuller. Fifteen cases were cited as precedents in the opinion.

On January 18, 1899, there came up before the Supreme Court a case[1] involving the constitutionality of the following Kansas statute:—

"SECTION 1. *Be it enacted by the legislature of the State of Kansas:* That in all actions against any railway company organized or doing business in this State, for damages by fire, caused by the operation of said railroad, it shall be only necessary for the plaintiff in said action to establish the fact that said fire complained of was caused by the operating of said railroad, and the amount of his damages (which proof shall be *prima facie* evidence of negligence on the part of said railroad): Provided that in estimating the damages under this act, the contributory negligence of the plaintiff shall be taken into consideration.

SECTION 2. In all actions commenced under this act, if the plaintiff shall recover, there shall be allowed him by the court a reasonable attorney's fee, which shall become a part of the judgment." [2]

In the Ellis Case, the claim was for $50 for the killing of a colt by the railroad company, the lower courts assessing an attorney's fee of $10. In this case, which we shall call the Matthews Case, the damages allowed from loss by fire caused by the railroad were $2094 and the attorney's fees assessed at $225. The railroad company set up the claim, on the basis of the decision in the Ellis Case as a precedent, that the provision relat-

[1] Atchison, Topeka & Santa Fe R. R. *v.* Matthews, 174 U. S. 96.

[2] Kansas Session Laws, 1885, Chap. 155, p. 258.

ing to the attorney's fees was a violation of the "due process of law" and the "equal protection" clauses of the Fourteenth Amendment. The Supreme Court by a majority opinion held the Kansas statute to be a valid enactment, distinguishing it from the Texas statute, which was declared unconstitutional in the Ellis Case. Mr. Justice Brewer again delivered the majority opinion, and with him concurred Mr. Chief Justice Fuller, and Justices Gray, White, and Shiras. Thirty-one cases were cited as precedents in the opinion.

There was a strong dissenting opinion by Mr. Justice Harlan, with whom concurred Justices Brown, Peckham, and McKenna. Thirty-five cases were cited as precedents in the opinion. In speaking of the two cases Mr. Justice Harlan said: "Placing the present case beside the former case, I am not astute enough to perceive that the Kansas statute is consistent with the Fourteenth Amendment, if the Texas statute be unconstitutional." [1]

Both of these statutes are essentially the same. It appears to the writer that the Texas statute is even more safely constitutional under the Amendment than the Kansas statute, in that it throws around the railroad company more safeguards and protection.

In looking over these two cases, it will be noticed that the position taken by Justices Harlan, Brown, and Peckham against the constitutionality of both statutes, and the position of Mr. Chief Justice Fuller, and Justices Gray and White in favor of the constitutionality of

[1] 174 U. S. 111.

both statutes, remains the same in each instance. Mr. Justice Field, who decided with the majority in the Ellis Case against the Texas statute, was no longer on the bench in the Matthews Case, his place being supplied by Mr. Justice McKenna, who decided with the minority in the Matthews Case against the Kansas statute. The new position taken by Justices Brewer and Shiras in the Matthews Case means, if not a reversal of the majority opinion in the Ellis Case, at least considerable confusion as to what legislation the people of the States may adopt along these lines.

The above illustration is a fair example of the futility of proposing that we wait until the Fourteenth Amendment be defined by the operation of the principle of *stare decisis*. Each side — not of the attorneys — but of the members of the Supreme Court itself, cited numerous precedents. If precedents could establish the law under the Amendment, both sides were right in each case.

We may not expect a definition of the "due process of law" and the "equal protection of the laws" clauses of the Fourteenth Amendment. They are too vague and too elastic. This weakens the doctrine of *stare decisis* to the point where it no longer becomes authoritative. It thus leads to confusion instead of serving as a guide. The business interests do not know what laws the State may enact concerning them. The people of the States do not know how far they can go in their attempts to solve their own economic and social problems. The Fourteenth Amendment, uncertain in its scope from the day of its adoption, remains uncertain. Under the present rules of procedure there is no escape from the dilemma.

Chart No. IV

SUMMARY TABLE SHOWING CERTAIN PHASES OF THE OPERATION OF THE FOURTEENTH AMENDMENT IN RELATION TO *STARE DECISIS*

October term	Number of opinions	Due process of law clause involved		Equal protection clause involved	Dissenting opinions	October term	Number of opinions	Due process of law clause involved		Equal protection clause involved	Dissenting opinions
		Liberty	Property					Liberty	Property		
1872	2	1	1	1	2	1893	15	2	10	6	2
1873	1		1			1894	9	5	2	3	2
1874	1					1895	14	8	8	7	4
1875	4	1	2	2	1	1896	26	7	20	9	6
1876	1		1	1	1	1897	20	7	14	13	5
1877	4		4	1	1	1898	31	1	28	14	14
1878	0					1899	31	4	23	10	5
1879	5	2	1	4	2	1900	32	6	20	16	13
1880	1			1	1	1901	25	3	17	14	5
1881	2		2	1		1902	28	5	16	14	8
1882	4		1	3	2	1903	31	10	24	14	5
1883	5	1	3		3	1904	34	6	23	10	15
1884	5	2	3	1		1905	38	8	24	14	10
1885	7		5	4	1	1906	35	8	28	15	7
1886	4	1	2	3	1	1907	36	6	7	16	9
1887	12	2	8	8	3	1908	30	10	25	12	8
1888	8	1	7	4	2	1909	28	7	20	13	8
1889	10	1	8	7	2	1910	30	8	25	20	3
1890	13	10	6	2	2						
1891	12	2	9	5	2						
1892	10	1	5	4		Total	604	128	423	273	155

CHAPTER IX

The Corporations and the Twilight Zone

The great problems facing the nation when the Fourteenth Amendment was being adopted were social and political rather than economic in the narrower sense of the word. The debates in Congress, the discussions in the various State legislatures, and the political campaigns before the people in 1866 and 1868 clearly reveal the motives underlying the making of that provision. It was a part of the great problem of reconstruction and had for its immediate purpose social and political readjustment in the South according to the theories of the party in power. It was a war amendment in that it attempted to conserve the results of the victory.

In so far as the strictly economic element was present, it was a matter of individual property rights — the protection of the weak and the oppressed. The object of protection was primarily the negro race. It was also intended to give protection to such of those from the North who had moved into the South immediately after the War. There was never any fear in the minds of the people of the North that their own States could not or would not protect their citizens in the common enjoyment of those rights and privileges which were the sacred heritages of all people of English stock. It never entered the public discussion, for instance, that the State of Massachusetts, or that the State of New York, would deprive persons within their bounds of life, liberty, or property without due process of law, or deny to them the equal protection of the laws.

There were no great corporation problems before the nation forty-five years ago. There were, of course, corporations and great activity in railroad building, but these economic movements were then in their infancy as compared with their modern status. The motive of the people for adopting the Fourteenth Amendment as a part of the Constitution of the United States was unrelated to the corporations.[1]

The actual operation of the Amendment reveals many interesting and some startling facts. The accompanying chart shows the distribution of litigation under the Amendment since its adoption to the beginning of the October Term, 1911.[2] In 1886 the Supreme Court declared a corporation to be a person within the meaning of the equal protection clause of the Amendment. This was in the case of

[1] "The Fourteenth Amendment was framed to protect the negroes from oppression by the whites, not to protect corporations from oppression by the legislature. It is doubtful whether a single one of the members of Congress who voted for it had any conception that it would touch the question of corporate regulation at all."—Arthur T. Hadley in the *Independent*, Vol. LXIV, pp. 836–837.

[2] See Chart No. V, p. 138.

Santa Clara County *v.* The Southern Pacific Railroad Co.[1] The question of the violation of the Fourteenth Amendment was presented to the Court, but the decision was made upon other grounds. However, the following preliminary announcement was made by Mr. Chief Justice Waite: "The Court does not wish to hear argument on the question whether the provision in the Fourteenth Amendment to the Constitution, which forbids a State to deny to any person within its jurisdiction the equal protection of the laws, applies to these corporations. We are all of the opinion that it does."

In 1888, in Pembina Mining Co. *v.* Pennsylvania,[2] this announcement was affirmed as a part of the decision. In 1889, in Minneapolis & St. L. R. R. Co. *v.* Beckwith,[3] the Supreme Court of the United States for the first time squarely and positively decided that a corporation was a person within the meaning of both the "due process of law" and the "equal protection of the laws" clauses of the Fourteenth Amendment. These cases, considered together as one opinion, mark one of the most important developments in our constitutional history. In an address in 1908 before the University of Berlin, President Hadley of Yale University declared them to rank with the Dartmouth College Case in their restraining effect upon the States

[1] 118 U. S. 394. Three cases were argued as one. One other railroad was involved.

[2] 125 U. S. 181.

[3] 129 U. S. 26.

in relation to the corporations. They opened the door for organized capital to contest whatever laws of the State it considered disadvantageous.

It will be noticed that out of six hundred and four opinions handed down under the Amendment, three hundred and twelve have involved a corporation as the principal party. Since 1889 litigation has greatly increased under the Amendment, averaging more than thirty cases a year for the last thirteen years. Corporations as parties seeking relief have increased in number until now more than two-thirds of all litigation under the Amendment is instituted in their behalf. On the other hand, questions involving the negro race, although never large, have dwindled down to an average of about one case each year.

Nearly all the important cases under the Amendment are in some way concerned with the question of State regulation of the corporations. During the life of the Amendment there have been fifty-five cases decided adversely to the States. Thirty-nine of these instances of Federal intervention have been in favor of a corporation; that is to say, about seventy-eight per cent. These include attempted regulation, by the several States involved, of telephone and gas rates; certain phases of the insurance business; railroad improvements, railroad profits, and freight and passenger rates; taxation and charter fees for public service companies; anti-trust laws; and the conservation of natural resources. It will thus be seen that the Amendment has taken on a new vitality within recent years. It has become a part of the great question of the day, What shall we do with the corporations?

The public service companies have so increased in power and in the territorial extent of their operations that they have become impatient of the restraints of State laws. What may be urged by the people of a State as a measure of social reform, to them takes on the appearance of an attack on vested interests. These great organizations, having in their service well-trained lawyers, have been quick to seize upon every opportunity to check the activity of the States when their own interests are affected. Their method is one of persistent opposition. Having great financial resources, they enter the field of politics to prevent the enactment of any statute that may operate to their immediate disadvantage. If they here fail to stem the tide of public opinion, and laws are made which will reduce their profits, they immediately set to work to prevent the enforcement of such laws. In other words, they now start on the long and winding road of litigation. They appeal to the State courts and to the constitution of the State. If they fail to obtain the relief sought, they seek shelter under the Federal Constitution, invoking protection under the contract clause, the commerce clause, and the Fourteenth Amendment. The two former can only be invoked under certain definite conditions. The latter can nearly always be used as a means of appeal from the action of a State to the

Supreme Court of the United States. Witness the attack of the Pacific States Telephone and Telegraph Company on the Oregon initiative and referendum laws in the Supreme Court of the United States, one of the grounds being that they operated to deprive the company of the equal protection of the laws in contravention of the Fourteenth Amendment!

These corporations do not always resort to the State courts. If the law in question is of great and immediate consequence, they frequently obtain temporary injunctions in the Federal district courts restraining the State from enforcing the law until such a time as the Federal courts can pass on its constitutionality under the Amendment. This method of checking the State has been increasingly used within the last few years. It often creates great local excitement. Two years ago the State of Alabama, to use the words of its governor, was "on the verge of civil war," on account of the enforcement of its railroad rate laws being restrained. The district judge threatened to cite the governor for contempt of court, and the governor threatened to appoint a commission to inquire into the sanity of the judge! A similar situation existed in Minnesota not long ago when the attorney-general of the State was put in jail for contempt of court because he attempted to enforce the rate law regardless of the Federal injunction.

This discussion is closely allied with other questions of national interest, such as the regulation of interstate commerce and the reform of the Federal judiciary, but we wish here to emphasize the point that the whole situation is aggravated by this unforeseen operation of the Fourteenth Amendment. To the corporations, which can easily undergo the strain of months and years of litigation, it has become a sure measure of delay. If a law is claimed to be unreasonable or discriminatory, it can be taken to the Supreme Court of the United States for final decision. This usually takes from one to four years. If the case has also been fought through all the courts of the State, it may require a much longer time. Nine times out of ten the decision of the Supreme Court of the United States will be adverse to the corporation seeking relief and in favor of the validity of the State law in question. Nevertheless, the corporation has had the advantage of several years of delay. During this period of delay it operates along the old lines. Sometimes the opposition becomes weary and a compromise is effected. Sometimes the opposing party in interest is a private citizen who, being unable to continue the litigation, abandons the case in despair.

This may be illustrated by reference to a Texas case which came up for decision in 1896.[1] A statute of Texas regulated the collection of certain claims against railroads. A citizen of Texas had a colt killed by a train, for which he obtained judgment before a justice of the peace for $50 plus an attorney's fee of $10 as

[1] Gulf, Colo., & Santa Fe Ry. *v.* Ellis, 165 U. S. 150.

provided by the law. The controversy was over the $10 and the principle involved in its relation to the Fourteenth Amendment. The case was fought through all of the courts of the State and was then taken to the Supreme Court of the United States, where after the additional delay a decision was rendered. In the meantime, the man in Texas had naturally enough abandoned the case.

This phase of the operation of the Amendment works almost wholly to the benefit of the corporations and individuals of considerable wealth. A poor man cannot afford to claim protection under the Amendment. It is too expensive a process. This situation exists to the embarrassment — often to the humiliation — of the State. It is one of the discordant notes of our times to hear of a judge of an inferior Federal court tying up the governmental machinery of a great and historic State at the instance of a powerful corporation because he does not agree with the State legislature as to what reforms should be instituted.

The Fourteenth Amendment in its practical operation gives to the Federal Government no power of control. Congress is powerless under it to make any laws by way of regulating the internal affairs of the States. It does, however, give the Federal Government through the Supreme Court almost unlimited power of intervention. That this power has been sparingly exercised is due to the conservative interpretation of that instrument by the members of the Supreme

Bench. This intervention under the Amendment has a very remarkable effect. The State is checked or restrained along a certain line of activity. The Federal Government is powerless to go any further. Having restrained the State from acting, its authority ceases absolutely. Within the particular sphere in controversy, the State is also rendered powerless. Thus there is created a field in which business operations may be carried on over which neither the Federal Government nor the State can take any affirmative action. This has been fittingly called the Twilight Zone. Intervention under the Amendment has this inevitable result. Beyond the pale of the law there is seen a shadowy realm in which the powers of wealth may move to and fro unhampered by the will of the people.

Let us illustrate this by a few striking examples. In the case of Smyth *v.* Ames [1] the Federal Supreme Court restrained, by virtue of the Fourteenth Amendment, the enforcement of the Nebraska freight rate law, on the ground that the rates were too low and discriminatory. Since this did not involve the question of interstate commerce, the Federal Government was powerless to come in and fix the proper rate or to advise the people of the State as to what would be considered a reasonable rate. Granting that the existing rates were too high, allowed the railroads too much profits, and consequently worked to the detriment of the welfare of the State, there was left no remedy

[1] 169 U. S. 466.

to the people who were thus directly affected. The Federal Government was helpless. The hands of the State were tied. The freight trains moved on in the Twilight Zone.

In the case of Buck *v.* Beach,[1] a man in New York owned certain notes which were payable in Ohio. The amount involved was $750,000. The notes were sent to an agent in Indiana. The State of Indiana placed a tax on them of $36,357.71. This was declared void by the Supreme Court of the United States under the Amendment, on the ground that the State of Indiana had no jurisdiction over them. They could not be taxed in Ohio or in New York, because they were located in Indiana. The Court has several times declared State taxes void which were assessed against a citizen on personal property which was situated in another State. The Federal Government could not tax these notes. In other words, they could not be taxed at all. They were sheltered in the shadows of the Twilight Zone.

Let us take one other illustration. In Lochner *v.* New York,[2] the Supreme Court of the United States declared void under the Amendment a law of the State of New York which limited the period of labor in bakeries to sixty hours per week. On a six-day basis this would be ten hours a day. Now the Federal Government has no power to regulate the hours of labor in New York. That is a State affair, the Federal

[1] 206 U. S. 392. [2] 198 U. S. 45.

Government being possessed of only delegated powers. This was a matter of local concern and had gained the favor of all branches of the local government. The Legislature had passed the law in response to the desire of the people who elected them; the highest court of the State had declared it valid; and the executive branch of the government was prepared to enforce it. All of this effort is brought to naught by a decision of the Federal Supreme Court declaring that such a law contravened the Fourteenth Amendment in that it interfered with the liberty of contract. The result is inevitable. The factories which bake bread for the people of New York may do their work with weary bodies and tired hands, beyond the reach of the law — Federal or State. The people of New York must eat this bread, their opinion that its method of manufacture is unsanitary to the contrary notwithstanding. The bakeries knead on in the Twilight Zone.

Every instance of Federal intervention under the Amendment creates a situation similar to the above and widens that shadowy sphere where business operations may go on unmolested either by the Federal Government or by the State. Every appeal to the Supreme Court of the United States under the Amendment, even though the sought-for intervention is denied, is conducive for a period of two or three years to the same result. Such delay is, in effect, temporary Federal intervention. It gives an air of uncertainty to the State law involved. The people of the State must in each case wait until the Federal Supreme Court has rendered its decision.

There is another phase of the Twilight Zone which may not here be discussed at length. It is wider in its reach than that created by the Fourteenth Amendment, but its shadows are not so dark. It is caused by Federal intervention in the affairs of the State under the Interstate Commerce Clause of the Constitution. There is a well-defined theoretical difference between the two. Under the Amendment the Federal Government can only intervene; under the commerce clause the Federal Government can both intervene and correct. For example, if the Supreme Court restrains the enforcement of a State law on the ground that it places a burden on interstate commerce, other branches of the Federal Government have the power to remedy the situation by affirmative action. Congress has the power to dispel the shadows of the Twilight Zone under the commerce clause by reducing the matter to a state of certainty by remedial legislation. Practically, however, the state of affairs remains to-day almost as hopeless as under the Fourteenth Amendment.

Thus we see that the Fourteenth Amendment, although a humanitarian measure in origin and purpose, has been within recent years practically appropriated by the corporations. It was aimed at restraining and checking the powers of wealth and privilege. It was to be a charter of liberty for human rights against property rights. The transformation has been rapid and complete. It operates to-day to protect the rights of property to the detriment of the rights of man. It has become the Magna Charta of accumulated and organized capital.

Chart No. V

TABLE SHOWING PARTIES SEEKING RELIEF FROM STATE ACTIVITY UNDER THE FOURTEENTH AMENDMENT

October Term U.S. Supreme Court	Total opinions	Corporations	Negro race	Individuals	October Term U.S. Supreme Court	Total opinions	Corporations	Negro race	Individuals	October Term U.S. Supreme Court	Total opinions	Corporations	Negro race	Individuals
1872	2	1	0	1	1885	7	3	0	4	1898	31	26	0	5
1873	1	0	0	1	1886	4	1	0	3	1899	31	18	2	11
1874	1	0	0	1	1887	12	5	0	7	1900	32	14	0	18
1875	4	1	1	2	1888	8	2	0	6	1901	25	14	0	11
1876	1	1	0	0	1889	10	4	1	5	1902	28	11	3	14
1877	4	1	0	3	1890	13	0	0	13	1903	31	13	2	16
1878	0	0	0	0	1891	12	8	0	4	1904	34	20	0	14
1879	5	0	3	2	1892	10	3	0	7	1905	38	19	1	18
1880	1	0	1	0	1893	15	9	0	6	1906	35	21	1	13
1881	2	0	0	2	1894	9	5	1	3	1907	36	19	0	17
1882	4	1	2	1	1895	14	5	4	5	1908	30	15	2	13
1883	5	1	1	3	1896	26	17	0	9	1909	28	20	2	6
1884	5	2	0	3	1897	20	9	1	10	1910	30	23	0	7
Totals											604	312	28	264

CHAPTER X

The Failure of the Fourteenth Amendment as a Constitutional Ideal

There is a feeling abroad in America that when a given measure becomes a part of the Constitution of the United States, its virtue must never henceforth be questioned. There is here a tendency towards a paper worship which involves a fundamental misconception of the true nature of constitutional law. The organic law of a people can never become fixed or static until the civic life of that people has ceased to develop, and become stagnant. This latter condition never exists, because every community is a living community and life always means motion and progress.

Notwithstanding the prevalence of this abnormal reverence for the letter of the Constitution, the American people are second to none in progressive activity and have gone beyond all in their practical view of life. This is a live country. The development of its political life has kept pace with its marvellous industrial achievements. Bold experiments in the realm of government have been launched without the guide of precedents. With an independence worthy of a free people, new conditions of life have been met with new political measures. The organic laws of the new frontier States in the West have been made to express the living ideals of the people. In general the State constitutions are frequently changed to meet the growing needs of each succeeding generation.

The same general principles which govern the State constitutions apply also to the fundamental law of the nation. It behooves each generation to examine for itself the political and constitutional ideals which form the basis of the Federal Government. There may not always be the necessity for a change in the organic law. There is the necessity for reëxamination and reëvaluation. Our fathers met their problems of constitutional law and solved them in the light of their own day. No less a burden has fallen upon their children. The Constitution is the servant of the people, not their master. *Salus populi est suprema lex.*

It is in this spirit that we approach this discussion of the Fourteenth Amendment to the Constitution of the United States. It has now been in operation forty-one years. We of the younger generation can look back on the history of its adoption without the bias of partisan zeal. The time has now come when we can see more clearly the whole movement of which this amendment formed a part. We can now ask what function it has performed as a constitutional measure. We can, by looking over its judicial history, see wherein it fails to meet the needs of this generation.

It would be but the vain discussion of an academic

question to hold up to criticism the adoption of the Amendment were it not for the fact that the purpose and manner of its adoption are closely related to its evaluation as a constitutional ideal. A study of the history of the adoption of the Fourteenth Amendment reveals certain forces at work which, according to the American ideal of a constitution, would render it an anomaly in the history of constitution making. It was a radical measure. Section one was a revolutionary departure from the original constitutional ideal. It was an abrupt break with the past. This was inevitable, because that section was intended to represent the results of the most radical of all proceedings — civil war. Yet a constitution formed at such a time must necessarily fail to express the normal life of the people.

The physical condition of the country was highly abnormal. Devastation and death were everywhere in evidence. The social, economic, and political life of the people was wrested from its natural channel. The social mind was wrought up to a high pitch of excitement. Brother had fought against brother, and the anger had not cooled. Intermingled with the voice of debate could be heard cries for revenge and groans of suppressed hatred and despair. It was not a time for the making of a constitutional measure which should govern the future of the whole country.

The method of its adoption was equally abnormal. It is not that the victorious North did not have the right to use abnormal and extra-legal methods in dealing with the conquered territory. They could be illogical if they chose. To say that the use of the Federal army in securing the adoption of the Amendment in the South was illegal, is of little force, since the North itself had the power to adopt the Amendment and then force each former seceding State to submit to it as it was readmitted into the Union. But the fact remains that the method was abnormal. The South was considered in the Union *de jure*. The South, *de facto*, adopted the Amendment in 1868, State by State. But since the white people of intelligence and property were disfranchised, the real South, which had rejected the Amendment in 1866, was unalterably opposed to that constitutional measure. How could it then be expected, when the life of the Southern people should have returned to its normal channel, that the Amendment should perform a natural function in their midst? It would be a fundamental weakness in any constitutional measure that the people to be most affected by it should have no voice in its adoption. This weakness is augmented if these people are proud and free, live together in one section of the country, and are opposed to the adoption of such a constitution.

Constitutional law cannot be superimposed upon a people accustomed to self-government. It must grow up from the bottom. Herein the adoption of the Amendment was undemocratic. It was an attempt by one section of the country to force its political ideals upon another section. The whole South and the border States, to say nothing of Ohio, New Jersey, Oregon, and California, expressed their disapproval. The Fourteenth Amendment did not represent the deliberate expression of the will of the whole people. It was forced into the Constitution of the United States before it had wrought itself into the constitution of the American people. It was not an outgrowth of the common life.

The Fourteenth Amendment expressed no new ideals of law and justice. The guarantees of its first section are as old as Magna Charta. They were embodied in the State constitutions before the original Federal Constitution was adopted. At the time of the adoption of the Amendment these constitutional ideals were expressed in every State constitution in the Union and were regarded as sacred heritages from our Anglo-Saxon forbears. The one new thing about the Amendment in this particular was that it shifted the guarantor from the State to the Federal Government. The States were not considered strong enough or safe enough to see that the fundamental guarantees of their constitutions were enforced. It was a reaction from the States' Rights theory. In effect, it was a repudiation of popular government. Whether such a step was then justified need not now be questioned, but whether it is valid for our own day is a matter of present interest.

The greatest weakness revealed in the history of the adoption of the Fourteenth Amendment lies in the fact that it was purely a party measure. It represented the ideals of the radical wing of the Republican Party. This was made no secret. On the contrary, it was a matter of pride to the Republican Party that they gained the victory by their own strength. All told, the fight lasted nearly three years, during which time the Democratic Party, North and South, opposed the Amendment to a man. So far as the records show, not one single Democrat in a single State of the Union voted in favor of the adoption of the Amendment. This cannot be said of any portion of the older constitutional amendments. Many Democrats voted for the adoption of the Thirteenth Amendment, and party lines were not strictly drawn on any of the previous twelve amendments or on the original Federal Constitution. An amendment to the organic law of the nation should be broad enough to appeal to the best element of all parties. Otherwise it will necessarily be defective in its operation.

In this summary of the history of the adoption of the Fourteenth Amendment we have seen that it was a radical measure growing out of an abnormal situation and adopted by abnormal and extra-legal methods. We turn now to practical considerations. We have before us the judicial history of the Amendment from 1868 to the present time, and we are in a position to enter into a critical study of its operation in the life of the nation. What function does it perform, and what is the sphere of its operation?

One of the first criticisms that presents itself is that the Amendment is abnormal in its operation. Private corporations are using it as a means to prevent the enforcement of State laws. Since 1891 a majority of cases under the Amendment have involved a corporation as the principal party. Out of a total of six hundred and four opinions by the Supreme Court since 1868 involving the Amendment, three hundred and twelve have been concerned with the corporations. The increase of this kind of litigation runs parallel to the rise of the trust movement in America. At the 1909–1910 term of the Court, out of a total of twenty-six opinions rendered under the Amendment, twenty involved a corporation as the principal party.

The Fourteenth Amendment was not adopted to protect the corporations from State reforms. The great principles of English liberties therein enunciated had in mind the protection of the individual from oppression. Now we hear the criticism that it is operating to shield the oppressor of the people. It was adopted to protect the individual from the tyranny of his State; it is operating to prevent the State from shielding its people. In 1868 there was no great corporation problem. The complex economic situation which we face to-day is of modern — almost sporadic — development. Organized capital has seized upon every device to strengthen its hands. The Fourteenth Amendment is the easiest of all constitutional measures to invoke. In a country where economic activity is so intense and time so vital an element, it has been grasped as a sure measure of delay, with always the possibility of obtaining affirmative relief. The Amendment, though intended primarily as a protection to the negro race, has in these latter days become a constitutional guarantee to the corporations that no State action toward them can become effective until after years of litigation through the State and Federal courts to the Supreme Court of the United States. The course of the Amendment is running far away from its originally intended channel. Of all the cases under the Amendment before the Supreme Court during the past forty-three years, only twenty-eight opinions involved the negro race question. A large majority of these were either frivolous or otherwise unimportant.

The Fourteenth Amendment gives to the Federal Government undefined and illimitable control over every phase of State activity. It throws into the hands of the Supreme Court of the United States more power over the States than does all the rest of the Constitution combined. Federal control exclusive of the Fourteenth Amendment is already of vast proportions. A mere enumeration of some of the separate grants of power affecting State relations and of prohibitions on the States calls to mind tremendous possibilities. For example, the power to regulate commerce among the several States; to establish post-offices and post-roads; to have complete jurisdiction and control over all Federal property in the several States. No State can, without the consent of Congress, lay any duties on imports or exports, or any duty of tonnage, or divide itself into two or more States. No State can enter into any treaty, alliance, or confederation; coin money; emit bills of credit; pass any bill of attainder or *ex post facto* law; or law impairing the obligation of contracts; or grant any title of nobility. Full faith and credit shall be given in each State to the public acts, records, and judicial proceedings of every other State. The citizens of each State shall be entitled to all of the privileges and immunities of the citizens in the several States. To these may be added the Thirteenth Amendment, prohibiting slavery, and the Fifteenth Amendment, which forbids the denial of the right to vote in any State on account of race, color, or previous condition of servitude.

This array of special powers and prohibitions would seem enough to give the Federal Government ample control over the affairs of the States. But in addition to all of these, the Fourteenth Amendment adds, "No State shall make or enforce any law which shall abridge the privileges or immunities of citizens of the United States; nor shall any State deprive any person of life, liberty, or property, without due process of law; nor deny to any person within its jurisdiction the equal protection of the laws." This one sentence, even under the present conservative interpretation given it by the Supreme Court, makes it the duty of that tribunal to pass judgment upon every form of

State activity — legislative, executive, administrative, or judicial — which may be brought into question by any person. It is not required that such a person be a citizen of the State. A foreign corporation comes under this provision. This is carrying Federal supervision to an extreme unthinkable to the founders of our government and is detrimental to the normal development of our people. It is too great an inroad on the police power of the State. Local self-government lies at the very foundation of a free country. The private affairs of a community should be regulated by that community without interference from the Federal Government so long as national interests are not directly affected. This ideal of local government is one of our most precious heritages from an heroic past. It is the school in which self-control, independence, and liberty are bred.

This is not a question of bringing to life a dead States' Rights doctrine. It is dealing with a fundamental principle of political science. It is by no means a dead issue. On the contrary, no student of public affairs can fail to see that the question of the relation of State functions to Federal control is one of the most vital problems in our body politic. These United States cover a vast territory. From ocean to ocean and from the Lakes to the Gulf may be found almost every variety of soil and climate. Physical environment and historical traditions have given rise to a diversity of custom and manner, thought and speech. The occupations of the people of the different sections are characterized by fundamental and permanent differences. While we are essentially one people along broadly nationalistic lines, one meets with a variety of local conditions and habits of life as one journeys from Maine to California or from Key West to Oregon. This very diversity makes local government essential to justice. The Supreme Court at Washington should not be required to pass upon these local questions. They should not be allowed to go beyond the supreme court of the State. Where the Federal courts interfere in the private affairs of a State to restrain a movement upheld by public opinion in that State, it is a blow to popular government and tends to breed disrespect and contempt among the people for Federal authority. The independence of the State governments needs to be encouraged, not discouraged. The weakness of our State legislatures has become a byword amongst us. This weakness is augmented by the operation of the Fourteenth Amendment, which hovers over their every action. Every law which they enact may be brought to the bar of the Supreme Court of the United States for final adjudication. Under that amendment the State cannot exercise a single act of sovereign power. It invades her holy of holies. Her people cannot any longer govern themselves with independence and boldness.

The Fourteenth Amendment is a paternal measure. It is the introduction of the principle of paternalism among a people whose genius is foreign to such a political ideal. It has in it the germ which may retard their growth. Like all centralizing measures, it tends to reduce the life of the people to a dead level of uniformity. In such a vast territory as the United States, occupied by a people who for centuries have been accustomed to trust themselves in the regulation of their domestic affairs, the stimulus of local self-government is essential to their natural development. This supervisory effect of the Amendment is at present reduced to a minimum because the majority of the Supreme Court of the United States are composed of conservative jurists. In the hands of a Supreme Court with radical centralizing views the Fourteenth Amendment could become a rod of iron to beat the people of the United States into one consolidated empire whose word of law, in matters light as well as weighty, should emanate from Washington.

On what principle, then, does the Amendment rest? Does it proclaim any new ideal of liberty? We have seen that it does not. The laws of every State have always guaranteed to all persons that life, liberty, or property shall not be taken without due process of law and that every one should have the benefit of the equal protection of the laws. These old phrases, hallowed by many memories among all people of English stock, have always been cherished by the American people. Their incorporation into an amendment to the Constitution of the United States, prohibitory as to the States, proclaimed, not a new principle of liberty, but a new method of government. The States were considered too weak or too capricious to see that their own fundamental law was enforced within their borders. One can readily understand this feeling in 1866, but it is a different matter in 1912. The practical effect of the operation of the Amendment has been simply to shift the court of final appeal from the State to the Federal Supreme Court, thus bringing to Washington for solution local domestic problems which are often bound up with the geographical and social environment of a State more than a thousand miles away.

Logically and historically the State should be given the benefit of the doubt in these local matters. When the people of a State are confronted with a local condition and they enact laws to meet it which are upheld by the supreme court of that State, the matter is often carried on to the Supreme Court at Washington, where nine men, out of touch with the local situation, are compelled to decide it. This would seem perfectly plausible if abstract justice could be applied and all men could be made to see a problem in the same light. But there is no abstract — no perfect justice. What is right depends on the circumstances. The strongest argument for the futility of the Fourteenth Amendment in this regard is that in practically every case of moment, where the supreme court of a State was reversed under it during the past forty-one years, a part of the Supreme Court of the United States agreed with the State court. Sometimes this was by a decision of four against five, in which event the points of difference were so finely drawn that the final decision rested, not upon any great principle of law or justice, but upon the personal political bias or governmental ideals of the majority of the members of the national Supreme Bench. And this in face of the well-known principle laid down by that court itself that no State law should be declared unconstitutional unless it was manifestly so! If it were possible for the Court to adhere to that rule, it is hard to see how any State law could ever be declared null and void, granting to the people of the States patriotism in their motives and intelligence in their official action.

The Fourteenth Amendment imposes upon the Supreme Court an impossible task. In the nature of things that tribunal cannot settle the local problems which are constantly arising here and there throughout this Union.

This is not a plea for State sovereignty. The States of this Union were never sovereign. Neither is the Federal Government sovereign. Sovereignty is now and has always been inherent in the American people. They delegate and distribute sovereign power as they see fit. The Federal Government and the States have from time to time exercised such sovereign powers as have been given them by the people. To say that Appomattox settled forever the relations between the States and the Federal Government would be a contradiction of one of the fundamental principles of social evolution. Our national life is in process. We are growing in every direction. As we grow we change. Neither the States nor the Federal Government are the same as they were even a decade ago. We are continually adjusting ourselves to meet new conditions. The development of our vast natural resources, with all of the attendant circumstances of manufacture and immigration, is causing great internal changes in the life of the nation. Externally we are constantly changing our relations to meet the advance or decline of the nations of the earth. Still living in the vigor of our youth, we are the least static of all peoples. These very circumstances and conditions render forever alive the great fundamental problem of American democracy — the relation of the States to the Federal Government in their respective spheres of activity. The Fourteenth Amendment has been a vain attempt at a solution.

Another serious criticism that may be brought against the Amendment is that it is a burden — an increasing burden to the Supreme Court of the United States. The labors of that tribunal, since the adoption of our colonial policy after the war with Spain, have become more and more severe and difficult. Appeals from Hawaii, Porto Rico, and the Philippine Islands are coming up for final decision. The opening of the Panama Canal will create other new problems to be settled by judicial decision. Our increasing maritime activities are bringing up a larger number of appeals from the courts of admiralty. The rise of the trusts and the attempts at Federal control and the enormous increase of interstate commerce within recent years burden the Court with problems of the gravest nature. These are vital Federal questions, and, if the Supreme Court could devote all of its attention to their solution alone, it would still need more time than it now has at its disposal. Add to these questions the great amount of litigation before the Court under the Fourteenth Amendment, and we find the supreme tribunal of the nation groaning beneath a burden too heavy to bear. Each year there remains a larger number of cases on the docket untouched. The records of the appellate docket for the past ten years show that the Court disposes of an average of only four hundred and twenty-three cases per year. The number of cases disposed of remains about the same year by year. On the other hand, the number of cases docketed is constantly on the increase. At the 1909–1910 term of the court there remained undisposed of from the 1908–1909 term, four hundred and seventy-eight cases. Five hundred and three new cases were docketed during 1909–1910. Three hundred and ninety-five cases were disposed of, leaving five hundred and eighty-six cases untouched.

The 1911 term has begun with eight hundred cases left over from the previous years. Six hundred new cases will probably be added during the year. If four hundred cases are disposed of, there will remain one thousand cases with which the next term of the Court must begin.

Now the Fourteenth Amendment is the most fruitful source of litigation of any part of the Constitution, with the possible exception of the Interstate Commerce Clause. It brings before the Court hard and delicate problems. It also brings much that is frivolous. Federal questions may be raised under it in any inferior State or Federal court. The Supreme Court is now rendering about thirty opinions each term on such questions. While this is not a large figure in itself, yet when it is remembered that the Court disposes of a large number of cases without rendering formal opinions, these thirty cases assume a larger proportion to the actual work done by the Court. It would be within reasonable limits to say that they represent about twenty per cent of the entire business of the Court. They involve constitutional questions. No matter by whom or with what motive presented, it is the duty of the Court to give them careful consideration. This puts the Supreme Court at the mercy of ambitious and unscrupulous lawyers. For the last twenty years litigation under the Amendment has steadily increased, over five hundred opinions being delivered. More than one-half of these dealt with the relations of the States to private corporations in their midst.

During the early years of the operation of the Amendment the Supreme Court, seeing the trend of this litigation, openly rebelled against this bringing of the domestic affairs of the States before it for adjudication.

It commented more than once on the strange misconceptions then existing concerning the scope of the Amendment. These complaints and warnings proved futile, and the litigation continued to increase with great rapidity, until to-day it occupies this large share of the time and attention of the Court. From present indications it will continue to increase. The potential power of the Fourteenth Amendment has never been fathomed. Its capacity to induce litigation is far greater than the actual cases show. It is capable of unlimited expansion. It may be used to bring to the bar of the Supreme Court of the nation every act of every State in the Union, be it administrative, executive, judicial, or legislative.

Another weakness of the Fourteenth Amendment as a constitutional ideal is that its terms are vague and indefinite. It is not possible to give to them even a working definition. The Supreme Court has attempted no definition. Nobody knows what powers are given to the Federal Government by the words, "No State shall deprive any person of life, liberty, or property, without due process of law." The Supreme Court has repeatedly declared that it can only be defined by the operation of the doctrine of *stare decisis*. This means that only the points presented by concrete cases under the Amendment shall be decided, so that, by the process of inclusion and exclusion, the precedents thus accumulated will in the course of time define every phase of the Amendment. This is in accord with a long-established theory of English law, but it is an impossible ideal when applied to the Fourteenth Amendment. It would take centuries of litigation to accumulate enough precedents to establish a practical definition. We have seen that after more than forty years of the operation of this principle of *stare decisis* the Court can still say that what is due process of law under the Amendment depends on the circumstances.

The difficulty of defining the terms of the Amendment is fundamental and inherent. It is an attempt to formulate organic law. The Amendment seeks in a few vague phrases to give to the Federal Government supervisory power over every State in the Union in their attempts at the regulation of the changing customs and habits of life of their people. As a consequence, the Amendment under the operation of the rule laid down by the Supreme Court will always remain undefined. In the life of each commonwealth in the nation, each day brings its problems new and different from those of the past. No doctrine of precedents can ever define the channels through which the living social organism must express itself.

This uncertainty of the meaning of the Amendment is no mere theory. It is a practical reality. Not only are the people ignorant of its scope as a constitutional measure, but the justices of the Supreme Court itself cannot agree on definitions even when concrete cases are presented. The long line of dissenting opinions forms a striking commentary on this point. Within the past forty-three years the Court found itself divided on the question of Federal intervention under the Amendment one hundred and fifty-five times. This is more than one-fourth of the entire number of opinions rendered during that time under the Amendment and includes practically every important decision.

In conclusion, we ask the question, Does the operation of the Fourteenth Amendment measure up to the American ideal of efficiency? Its adoption set in operation a vast amount of governmental machinery. For forty-three years it has been before the American courts. Its judicial history is an open book. Has the effort been worth while? Does it serve to promote the peace and prosperity of the republic? Our study has shown that these questions must be answered in the negative. The amount of governmental activity under the Amendment is too great to justify the small results obtained. Out of six hundred and four cases in which opinions were delivered, fought through the several courts to the Supreme Court of the United States, only fifty-five were decided in favor of the person or corporation that invoked the Federal intervention against the States. Nine persons out of every ten fail to gain the relief sought under the Amendment. This tenth person is usually a corporation, as are also five of the other nine. The net results of the forty-three years of litigation under the Amendment are fifty-five instances of restraint upon State action. Some of these were of little or no importance; others involved questions of State procedure and may be considered as technical; and a few, more often with dissenting opinions, declared null and void important elements of State laws and constitutions.

It has cost the American people a large amount of time and money to obtain these meagre results. It is doubtful whether any good was accomplished. Some of the States, especially in the West, have been greatly humiliated by having their entire machinery of government tied up by the corporations under the Amendment. When the corporation comes out victorious, it is a doubtful victory. It is doubtful because it is gained at the expense of disappointment to the people of the State. It is a set-back to popular government. This operation of the Fourteenth Amendment runs counter to the ideals expressed in the preamble to the Constitution itself. It does anything but promote domestic tranquillity.

The Amendment is a stumbling-block to the American people. It stands in the way of many important local reforms. It weakens and sometimes abrogates the police power of the States, yet it gives no power to Congress to initiate affirmative legislation. As a centralizing measure it is hopelessly inefficient. Whatever may have been the intention of Congress in proposing the Amendment, as a practical means of Federal control it is wholly negative. Under its operation the Federal Supreme Court can restrain the States from acting in certain spheres, yet no branch of the Federal Government has the power to come in and do in a better way that which was proposed by the State. Herein the operation of the Fourteenth Amendment differs from that of the Interstate Commerce Clause of the Constitution. Under the latter the Federal Government can through Congress initiate affirmative legislation to remedy those evils which the State had proposed to remedy, but was restrained by the Federal courts. Under the Fourteenth Amendment the Federal Government can only restrain. It can propose no remedy of its own. It can suggest no remedy to the States.

Thus there has grown up what is now being called the Twilight Zone. It is a region between the States and the Federal Governments where commercial activity may go on without any governmental control. Those who operate there are outside of the pale of the law. The State is restrained by Federal authority from acting; the Federal Government is powerless to act. This Twilight Zone is greatly enlarged at present by the unsettled relations between the Federal Government and the States under the Interstate Commerce Clause of the Constitution. There is a possible remedy here, but as long as the Fourteenth Amendment remains a part of the Supreme Law of the Land, the Twilight Zone will ever be a shadow across the pathway of the American Republic.

The operation of the Fourteenth Amendment is an economic waste. It does not produce results commensurate with the efforts put forth. The actual money cost to the American people, to maintain the expense of litigation under the Amendment year by year, runs up into large sums. One of the chief effects of the operation of the Amendment is to afford a means of delay to those who can afford to spend years in litigation. The great corporations are here the chief beneficiaries. It is nearly always in order to raise the question of the violation of the Fourteenth Amendment in the lower courts. This always means a delay of perhaps two or three years, and delay — even in the face of an adverse decision to the supposed aggrieved party — is always an advantage, often a victory. It is one of the least criticisms to say that it is a waste of time and money for the government to attempt to maintain such a constitutional measure.

The primary purpose of the adoption of the Fourteenth Amendment was to elevate the negro to a plane of equality with the white people and to protect him in his newly given rights. In its attempts to carry out this ideal, Congress was effectually restrained by the Supreme Court. Consequently, as related to the negro race, the Amendment is negative and non-automatic. It has failed of its purpose because there is no Federal power to enforce it, and because the negroes have not been qualified to gain for themselves the ideals which it seeks to enforce. When they do become so qualified, they will have no need of the Fourteenth Amendment. Of the few cases reaching the Supreme Court of the United States within the past forty years involving the negro race question under the Amendment, in no single instance of importance has a State been restrained from enforcing its laws.

In closing these criticisms on the Fourteenth Amendment to the Constitution of the United States, it seems fitting to quote the words of Pelatiah Webster, which, although spoken in 1783, state a living and fundamental principle of jurisprudence: "Laws or ordinances of any kind (especially of august bodies of high dignity and consequence), which fail of execution, are much worse than none. They weaken the government, expose it to contempt, destroy the confidence of all men, native and foreigners, in it, and expose both aggregate bodies and individuals who have placed confidence in it to many ruinous disappointments which they would have escaped had no such law or ordinance been made.[1]

[1] Quoted from Hannis Taylor, Esq., *The Genesis of the Supreme Court*, in *Case and Comment* for June, 1911.

CHAPTER XI

Proposed Remedies

The foregoing studies into the history and the practical operation of the Fourteenth Amendment reveal to us a situation highly unsatisfactory and of positive harmful tendencies. It is evident that some remedial steps should be taken. It would be most natural to suggest the repeal of the Amendment, but on account of the inherent difficulty of amending the Federal Constitution and by reason of the peculiar sentiment which still lingers around the War amendments, its repeal at this time can hardly be considered practicable.

In order to attain the desired result it is not, however, absolutely necessary that the Amendment be repealed. In all cases arising under the Fourteenth Amendment the Supreme Court of the United States exercises only appellate jurisdiction. Under Article III, Section 2, of the Constitution it is the duty of Congress to provide for and regulate this appellate jurisdiction with such exceptions as seem fit and proper. The Supreme Court can exercise no appellate jurisdiction except in those cases thereby provided. This principle was recently restated by Mr. Justice Moody in St. Louis & Iron Mt. Ry. *v.* Taylor,[1] in which he said, "Congress

[1] 210 U. S. 292.

has regulated and limited the appellate jurisdiction of this Court over the State courts by Section 709 of the Revised Statutes, and our jurisdiction in this respect extends only to the cases there enumerated, even though a wider jurisdiction might be permitted by the constitutional grant of power." The constitutional grant here referred to was the Fourteenth Amendment. Section 709 of the Revised Statutes was enacted by Congress about fifty years ago and was recently reënacted to form Section 237 of the Judicial Code, which went into effect January 1, 1912. It reads as follows:—

"A final judgment or decree in any suit in the highest court of a State in which a decision in the suit could be had, where is drawn in question the validity of a treaty or statute of, or any authority exercised under, the United States, and the decision is against their validity; or where is drawn in question the validity of a statute of, or an authority exercised under any State, on the ground of their being repugnant to the Constitution, treaties, or laws of the United States, and the decision is in favor of their validity; or where any title, right, privilege, or immunity is claimed under the Constitution, or any treaty, or statute of, or commission held, or authority exercised under, the United States, and the decision is against the title, right, privilege, or immunity especially set up or claimed, by either party under such Constitution, treaty, statute, commission, or authority, may be reëxamined and reversed or affirmed in the Supreme Court upon a writ of error. The writ shall have the same effect as if the judgment or decree complained of had been rendered or passed in a court of the United States. The Supreme Court may reverse, modify, or affirm the judgment or decree of such State court, and may, at their discretion, award execution or remand the same to the court from which it was removed by the writ."

In addition to this jurisdiction over the States, the Supreme Court has, of course, appellate jurisdiction over all cases under the Fourteenth Amendment which have their origin in the inferior Federal courts. These, as we have seen, are comparatively few in number and consist chiefly of proceedings by way of injunctions, temporary or permanent, restraining the enforcement of State laws. They are, however, of prime importance. This jurisdiction is now regulated by Sections 262–266 of the Judicial Code.[1] Sections 262–265 are the re-enactments of Revised Statutes, Sections 716, 718, 719, and 720. Section 266 is new and supersedes the act of June 18, 1910. It went into effect January 1, 1912, and provides in effect that permanent injunctions restraining State activity may be issued by a Federal court only when the petition has been heard by three judges, one of whom must be a circuit judge or a justice of the Supreme Court. Five days' notice must be given to the State officials, and two of the three judges must concur in granting the application before the writ of injunction can be issued. It is, however, provided that a temporary injunction may be issued as heretofore by only one judge.

These laws could be amended by Congress in many ways either to increase or to decrease litigation under

[1] See Appendix A, p. 177.

the Fourteenth Amendment. For example, writs of error could be allowed to the party aggrieved in those cases where the courts of final jurisdiction in the States declare State laws violative of the Fourteenth Amendment. This would greatly increase the appellate jurisdiction of the Supreme Court under the Amendment. On the other hand, Congress could take away all such appellate jurisdiction from that tribunal by denying the right to writs of error to such State courts of final jurisdiction in all cases, and by denying to the Federal courts the power to issue writs of injunction against the States thereunder. This would, so long as such a law remained in force, amount to practically a repeal of the Amendment.

For practical reasons a middle ground is proposed, namely: —

1. Limit the right to writs of error to the State courts, under questions involving the Fourteenth Amendment, only to those cases where the State court of final jurisdiction is divided on the question; that is to say, not unanimous. If the State court of final jurisdiction is of the unanimous opinion that the State law or prodecure in question is not repugnant to the Fourteenth Amendment, then no writ of error shall be allowed.

2. Prohibit to the Federal district courts, or to any of the Federal district or circuit judges, the power to assume, by virtue of the Fourteenth Amendment, jurisdiction of any injunction, *habeas corpus*, or any

other high or extraordinary proceedings by way of restraint upon, or intervention into, the activities of the States.

3. Provide that no State law or procedure shall be declared unconstitutional by the Supreme Court of the United States as being repugnant to the provisions of the Fourteenth Amendment except by a unanimous opinion of that Court.

A bill has already been introduced in the Senate the provisions of which include the last-mentioned suggestion.[1]

Such amendments by Congress to existing statutes, though apparently radical, would be based upon both precedent and common sense and within the plain path of duty under the Constitution.

In Hodges *v.* U. S.,[2] the Court made the following observation: "Notwithstanding the adoption of these three Amendments the national government still remains one of enumerated powers, and the Tenth Amendment, which reads, 'the powers not delegated to the United States by the Constitution, nor prohibited by it to the States, are reserved to the States respectively, or to the people,' is not shorn of its vitality." But this is just what has occurred. The practical operation of the Fourteenth Amendment is both supplanting and devitalizing the Tenth Amendment.

It would be a different matter if the Fourteenth Amendment presented to the courts only questions of

[1] See Appendix D, p. 184. [2] 203 U. S. 1.

law, but this is not the case. As a rule, when the Supreme Court declares a State law unconstitutional under the Amendment, what it really does is not to decide a question of law, but a question of governmental policy. The real question is not whether the legislation is legal, but whether it is wise and expedient, the criterion of wisdom being the opinion of a majority of the Supreme Bench. This is substantially the same conclusion reached also independently by Professor Henry R. Seager [1] and by Professor Frank J. Goodnow [2] in recent studies.

Thus five men have the power to declare null and void, on the ground of governmental policy, a State law which is upheld by four members of the Supreme Court of the United States; the unanimous opinion of the Supreme Court of the State; the majority — or even unanimous — opinion of both houses of the State legislature; and by the public opinion of the State at large. Had there been a rule requiring the unanimous opinion of the Supreme Court before intervening in the affairs of a State, only twenty-four instances of restraint would have been thus put upon the States since the adoption of the Amendment, the most of them being of minor importance.

Now the Court has time and again expressly disavowed any intention of discussing or deciding matters

[1] *The Attitude of American Courts towards Restrictive Labor Legislation*, in *Pol. Sci. Quar.*, Vol. XIX, p. 589.

[2] *Social Reform and the Constitution*, p. 247.

of policy. It operates on the theory that its function is to decide only matters of law. This has been impossible to carry out in practice. Every question of constitutional law involves in itself a question of governmental policy, and the Court, under present rules of procedure, is in duty bound, in the last analysis, to decide whether the law in question is itself reasonable and wise.

To prescribe a rule requiring the Supreme Court to be unanimous in its opinion when declaring a State law unconstitutional under the Amendment would be in harmony with the principle upon which the Court is presumed to operate. In Munn *v.* Illinois,[1] the Court, through Chief Justice Waite, spoke as follows: "Every statute is presumed to be constitutional. The courts ought not to declare one to be unconstitutional unless it is clearly so. If there is doubt, the express will of the legislature should be sustained." Again, in Halter *v.* Nebraska,[2] Mr. Justice Harlan, speaking for the Court, said: "In our considerations of the questions presented we must not overlook certain principles of constitutional construction, long ago established and steadily adhered to, which preclude a judicial tribunal from holding a legislative enactment, Federal or State, unconstitutional and void, unless it be manifestly so." This is the settled doctrine of the Court.

Surely then a law is not clearly and manifestly unconstitutional when one or more of the members of the

[1] 94 U. S. 123. [2] 205 U. S. 40.

Court itself have serious doubts as to the question! Upon this principle laid down by the Court a State law could only be declared void when the opinion of the Court was unanimous. In practice the Court does not adhere to this principle. Apart from State laws declared unconstitutional by a majority opinion only, under other clauses of the Federal Constitution, there have been thirty-one such cases under the Fourteenth Amendment alone. These include the New York law regulating the hours of labor in bake shops, by a decision of five to four; the Oklahoma natural gas law, by a decision of six to three; the Kansas corporation charter fee law, by five to four; a similar law for Alabama and for Arkansas, each declared unconstitutional by a decision of six to three; railroad rate laws of Minnesota and Michigan, each also by six to three.[1] These are all cases of vast importance, and the dissenting opinions are not only replete with legal learning in advocating the validity of the State laws in question, but they also sound the notes of warning to the republic at the gradual encroachments of the Fourteenth Amendment. This is certainly evidence enough of the doubt of the unconstitutionality of such laws. The strongest criticisms of the Supreme Court of the United States in this regard come, not from the public or the press, but from the members of that Court itself.

As to the proposal to prohibit Federal injunctions altogether under and by virtue of the Amendment, only

[1] For these and further citations see Chapter VII.

a word need be said. We have elsewhere in this study attempted to show the evils of such practice. The frequent resort to this high and extraordinary procedure in the Federal courts gives evidence of a distrust of the State courts and of the people of the State. It is furthermore an attempt at a short cut to justice. Instead of seeking relief in the State courts, the Federal courts are resorted to that State action be immediately restrained. Chief Justice Fuller, in a dissenting opinion in Prentis *v.* Atlantic Coast Line,[1] in commenting on this situation, spoke as follows: "Power grows by what it feeds on, and to hold that State railroad companies can take their chances for fixing of rates in accordance with their views in a tribunal provided for that purpose by State constitutions and laws, and then if dissatisfied with the result, decline to seek a review in the highest court of the State, though possessed of the absolute right to do so, and invoke the power of Federal courts to put a stop to such proceedings, is in my opinion utterly inadmissible and of a palpably dangerous tendency." Mr. Justice Harlan concurred in these sentiments. Yet are we not driven to admit the melancholy fact that such procedure by the railroads has almost reached the dignity of established custom? It has become the ordinary thing for the railroad company to seek a Federal injunction against the State when the only question involved is the reasonableness of the intra-State rate.

[1] 211 U. S. 237.

The proposals to require unanimous opinions of the Supreme Court before declaring a State law unconstitutional, and the prohibition of Federal injunctions, under the Amendment, would give to the States greater protection and would insure the stability of their laws, but litigation under the Amendment would not necessarily decrease. There would remain the same motive for and the same possibility of delay. Writs of error to the State courts would be sought then as now — regardless of the fact that the chances of restraining State activity would be greatly lessened.

The other proposal — to limit the possibility of writs of error from the Supreme Court of the United States to the State courts of final jurisdiction, to those cases only in which such State courts are not unanimous in their opinion as to whether the Fourteenth Amendment has been violated by the State — would greatly decrease the possibility of future litigation. It would allow appellate proceedings to the Federal Supreme Court only in those cases where the State Supreme Court is in doubt as to the constitutionality of the law or procedure in question. This would not be radical legislation by Congress. It would be complementary to the laws already enacted. As has been shown, it is the duty of Congress to regulate, as it sees fit, the appellate jurisdiction of the Supreme Court. The laws now in force do not allow the aggrieved party to seek a writ of error from the Federal Supreme Court when the State Supreme Courts declare a law or procedure unconstitutional by virtue of the Fourteenth Amendment. State action is final when its highest court annuls a law as being repugnant to the Amendment, even though it does so by a bare majority.

In view of the undesirable character of the litigation under the Amendment at the present time, why not make State action final when the unanimous opinion of its highest court declares that the State law or procedure in question is not repugnant to the Amendment — that is to say, is just and reasonable? There is no real Federal question involved in either case. In the light of our constitutional history, it is perfectly clear that the present privilege of litigants to set up in the courts as Federal questions a vast array of purely local State problems, is almost entirely fortuitous and is contrary to the fundamental principles of our government.

The effect of enacting these or similar proposals into law would, by reducing the amount of litigation under the Amendment, relieve the Supreme Court of a great burden both of work and of an unsought and unwelcomed responsibility. It would lessen the time and expense of litigation. It would render the State laws more certain, both substantively and adjectively, thus clarifying the Twilight Zone. It would enable the State to provide with freedom and independence for the health, morals, and safety of its people and for their peace, happiness, prosperity, and common welfare.

It would bring us into a more consistent harmony with, not only the ideals of the founders of this republic, but also with the long line of Anglo-American constitutional achievement. It would, in a proper measure, restore home rule to the States.

APPENDICES

APPENDIX A

THE TEXT OF THE JUDICIAL CODE OF 1912 RELATING TO INJUNCTIONS

SECTION 262. The Supreme Court and the district courts shall have power to issue writs of *scire facias*, The Supreme Court, the circuit courts of appeals, and the district courts shall have power to issue all writs not specifically provided for by statute, which may be necessary for the exercise of their respective jurisdictions, and agreeable to the usages and principles of law.

SECTION 263. Whenever notice is given of a motion for an injunction out of a district court, the court or judge thereof may, if there appear to be danger of irreparable injury from delay, grant an order restraining the act sought to be enjoined until the decision upon the motion; and such order may be granted with or without security, in the discretion of the court or judge.

SECTION 264. Writs of injunction may be granted by any justice of the Supreme Court in cases where they might be granted by the Supreme Court; and by any judge of a district court in cases where they might be granted by such court. But no justice of the Supreme Court shall hear or allow any application for an injunction or restraining order in any cause pending in the circuit to which he is allotted, elsewhere than within such circuit, or at such place outside of the same as the parties may stipulate in writing, except when it cannot be heard by the district judge of the district. In case of the absence from the district of the district judge, or of his disability, any circuit judge of the circuit in which the district is situated may grant an injunction or restraining order in any case pending in the district court, where the same might be granted by the district judge.

SECTION 265. The writ of injunction shall not be granted by any court of the United States to stay proceedings in any court of a State, except in cases where such injunction may be authorized by any law relating to proceedings in bankruptcy.

SECTION 266. No interlocutory injunction suspending or restraining the enforcement, operation, or execution of any statute of a State by restraining the action of any officer of such State in the enforcement or execution of such statute, shall be issued or granted by any justice of the Supreme Court, or by any district court of the United States, or by any judge thereof, or by any circuit judge acting as district judge, upon the ground of the unconstitutionality of such statute, unless the application for the same shall be presented to a justice of the Supreme Court of the United States, or to a circuit or district judge, and shall be heard and determined by three judges, of whom at least one shall be a justice of the Supreme Court, or a circuit judge, and the other two may be either circuit or district judges, and unless a majority of said three judges shall concur in granting such application. Whenever such application as aforesaid is presented to a justice of the Supreme Court, or to a judge, he shall immediately call to his assistance to hear and determine the application two other judges: *Provided, however,* That one of such three judges shall be a justice of the Supreme Court, or a circuit judge. Said application shall not be heard or determined before at least five days' notice of the hearing has been given to the governor and to the attorney-general of the State, and to such other persons as may be defendants in the suit: *Provided,* That if of opinion that irreparable loss or damage would result to the complainant unless a temporary restraining order is granted, any justice of the Supreme Court, or any circuit or district judge, may grant such temporary restraining order at any time before such hearing and determination of the application for an interlocutory injunction, but such temporary restraining order shall remain in force only until the hearing and determination of the application for an interlocutory injunction upon notice as aforesaid. The hearing upon such application for an interlocutory injunction shall be given precedence and shall be in every way expedited and be assigned for a hearing at the earliest practicable day after the expiration of the notice hereinbefore provided for. An appeal may be taken direct to the Supreme Court of the United States from the order granting or denying, after notice and hearing, an interlocutory injunction in such case.

APPENDIX B

THE TEXT OF THE WAR AMENDMENTS

ARTICLE XIII

SECTION 1. Neither slavery nor involuntary servitude, except as a punishment for crime whereof the party shall have been duly convicted, shall exist within the United States, or any place subject to their jurisdiction.

SECTION 2. Congress shall have power to enforce this article by appropriate legislation.[1]

ARTICLE XIV

SECTION 1. All persons born or naturalized in the United States, and subject to the jurisdiction thereof, are citizens of the United States and of the State wherein they reside. No State shall make or enforce any law which shall abridge the privileges or immunities of citizens of the United States; nor shall any State deprive any person of life, liberty, or property, without due process of law; nor deny to any person within its jurisdiction the equal protection of the laws.

SECTION 2. Representatives shall be apportioned among the several States according to their respective

[1] Proclaimed to be in force December 18, 1865.

numbers, counting the whole number of persons in each State, excluding the Indians not taxed. But when the right to vote at any election for the choice of electors for President and Vice President of the United States, Representatives in Congress, the Executive and Judicial officers of a State, or the members of the Legislature thereof, is denied to any of the male inhabitants of such State, being twenty-one years of age, and citizens of the United States, or in any way abridged, except for participation in rebellion, or other crime, the basis of representation therein shall be reduced in the proportion which the number of such male citizens shall bear to the whole number of male citizens twenty-one years of age in such State.

SECTION 3. No person shall be a Senator or Representative in Congress, or elector of President and Vice President, or hold any office, civil or military, under the United States, or under any State, who, having previously taken an oath, as a member of Congress, or as an officer of the United States, or as a member of any State legislature, or as an executive or judicial officer of any State, to support the Constitution of the United States, shall have engaged in insurrection or rebellion against the same, or given aid or comfort to the enemies thereof. But Congress may by a vote of two-thirds of each House remove such disability.

SECTION 4. The validity of the public debt of the United States, authorized by law, including debts incurred for payment of pensions and bounties for services in suppressing insurrection or rebellion, shall not be questioned. But neither the United States nor any State shall assume or pay any debt or obligation incurred in aid of insurrection or rebellion against the United States, or any claim for the loss or emancipation of any slave; but all such debts, obligations, and claims shall be held illegal and void.

SECTION 5. The Congress shall have power to enforce, by appropriate legislation, the provisions of this article.[1]

ARTICLE XV

SECTION 1. The right of citizens of the United States to vote shall not be denied or abridged by the United States or by any State on account of race, color, or previous condition of servitude.

SECTION 2. The Congress shall have power to enforce this article by appropriate legislation.[2]

[1] Proclaimed to be in force July 28, 1868.
[2] Proclaimed to be in force March 30, 1870.

APPENDIX C

Chart No. VI

STATISTICAL SUMMARY OF OPINIONS DELIVERED UNDER THE FOURTEENTH AMENDMENT, 1868–1910

U. S. Supreme Court		Sphere of State Activity Involved				Federal Question Involved under 14th Amendment					Initial Jurisdiction		Final Disposition				Parties	
							Due Process of Law											
October Term	Number of Cases	Police Power	Eminent Domain	Taxation	Procedure	Priv. or Immun. of Citz.	Life	Liberty	Property	Equal Protection	State Court	Federal Court	Decision *pro* State	Decision *vs.* State	Merits not Decided	Dissenting Opinions	Private Corporation	Negro Race
1872	2				1	2		1	1	1	2		2			2	1	
1873	1	1				1			1		1		1					
1874	1	1				1					1		1					
1875	4	1		1	1	2		1	2	2	2	2	4			1	1	1
1876	1	1							1	1	1		1			1	1	
1877	4	2	2	1					4	1	4		4			1	1	
1878																		
1879	5	2		1	2	1	2	2	1	4	4	1	3	2		2		3
1880	1	1								1	1			1		1		1
1881	2	1		1					2	1	2		2					
1882	4	2			1				1	3	3	1	3	1		2	1	2
1883	5	2		1	2		1	1	3		4	1	5		1	3	1	1
1884	5	3	2					2	1	3	5		5				2	
1885	7	3		1	3	1			5	4	7	1	5	2		1	3	
1886	4	3		1				1	2	3	4	1	4			1	1	
1887	12	10			3	1	2	2	8	8	12	2	12		1	3	5	
1888	8	4		1	3	1		1	7	4	8		8		1	2	2	
1889	10	3		3	4	2		1	8	7	10	1	9	1	1	2	4	1
1890	13	8			5		3	10	6	2	13	3	13		1	2		
1891	12	9		2	3		2	2	9	5	11	1	12		1	2	8	
1892	10	4	1	1	4		2	1	5	4	9	3	10		1		3	
1893	15	9	1	2	3	4	1	2	10	6	14	1	13	2	3	2	9	
1894	9	6		1	3		1	5	2	3	7	2	9		1	2	5	1
1895	14	7	2	2	4	1	1	8	8	7	10	4	14		2	4	5	4
1896	26	13	2	5	6			7	20	9	24	2	22	4	6	6	17	
1897	20	7	1	7	5	2	2	7	14	13	16	5	18	2	3	5	9	1
1898	31	11	1	15	4	1		1	28	14	30	1	28	3	9	14	26	
1899	31	15	2	6	8	3	2	4	23	10	26	5	28	3	11	5	18	2
1900	32	12		13	8	1	2	6	20	16	25	7	31	1	8	13	14	
1901	25	11		10	5	2	2	3	17	14	21	4	23	2	5	5	14	
1902	28	10	2	7	11	3		5	16	14	25	3	26	2	8	8	11	3
1903	31	18		7	8	3		10	24	14	22	10	28	3	9	5	13	2
1904	34	12	4	11	10			6	23	01	25	9	28	6	4	15	20	
1905	38	23	1	7	7	1	1	8	24	14	25	13	36	2	7	10	19	1
1906	35	17	2	6	9	3		8	28	15	27	8	32	3	4	7	21	1
1907	36	20	1	9	9	4		6	27	16	30	6	31	5	6	9	19	
1908	30	16		4	10			10	25	12	21	9	28	2	12	8	16	2
1909	28	10	1	11	6			7	20	13	25	5	22	6	6	8	20	2
1910	30	24	2	5	0			8	25	20	20	10	28	2	1	3	23	
Total	604	302	27	144	146	40	24	128	423	273	497	121	549	55	112	155	313	28

APPENDIX D

POWER OF SUPREME COURT TO DECLARE ACTS OF CONGRESS UNCONSTITUTIONAL

THE purpose of this bill is not to allow one, two, three, or four members of the Supreme Court to overrule eight, seven, six, or five members of that distinguished branch of our government, but, rather, to enable one, two, three, or four members of that court to prevent eight, seven, six, or five members from overruling the wishes of the nation as expressed through Congress or the wishes of a sovereign State as expressed by its electorate or by its legislature.

REMARKS OF HON. JONATHAN BOURNE, JR., OF OREGON, IN THE SENATE OF THE UNITED STATES, MONDAY, AUGUST 14, 1911

Mr. BOURNE said : —

Mr. PRESIDENT : I introduce a brief bill and will ask to have it read in order that it may appear in the *Congressional Record.*

The bill (S. 3222) to provide rules for speedy and final decision of questions concerning the constitutionality of national and State laws and constitutional provisions and for the interpretation and construction of the Federal laws and Constitution was read the first time at length, as follows : —

Be it enacted, etc., That in any action, suit, or proceeding in the Supreme Court of the United States when the constitutionality of any provision of a Federal or State law, or of a State constitution, shall be drawn in question or decided, the constitutionality thereof shall be sustained unless the Supreme Court, by unanimous decision of all its members qualified to sit in the cause, shall determine that the provision in controversy is not authorized or is prohibited by the Constitution of the United States. That in any action, suit, or proceeding in the Supreme Court when the meaning, interpretation, or construction of any language of any Federal law or of the Constitution of the United States shall be drawn in question or decided, the same shall be interpreted and construed literally as the words are commonly understood in everyday use, unless the Supreme Court, by unanimous decision of all its members qualified to sit in the cause, shall decide that such literal interpretation is not the true expression of the legislative intention and meaning in the language in controversy.

SECTION 2. If any inferior Federal court, commission, or tribunal shall decide in any case that any provision of any such Federal or State law or provision of a State constitution is not authorized or is prohibited by the Constitution of the United States, or shall interpret or construe the meaning of any language of any Federal law or constitutional provision to be different from its literal verbal statements as the words are commonly understood in everyday use, it shall be the duty of said lower court, commission, or tribunal to forthwith certify said question of constitutionality, meaning, interpretation, or construction to the Supreme Court of the United States for final decision. Every such Federal inferior court, commission, and tribunal is hereby authorized, in the discretion of the members thereof, to certify any such question to the Supreme Court of the United States for decision in advance of the trial of the cause on the merits in said lower court, commission, or tribunal. The United States Department of Justice shall pay all the necessary expenses and costs of presenting every such question in the Supreme Court of the United States. It shall be the duty of the Supreme Court to advance every such cause over all other causes on the docket not directly involving the constitutionality, meaning, interpretation, or construction of any such act, law, or constitutional provision.

Mr. BOURNE. Mr. President, I shall not at this time present an argument upon this bill. The purpose of the measure will, I think, be readily apparent. The Congress of the United States is one of the coördinate branches of our government. A very considerable number of the Members of both Houses of Congress are learned in the law, and some of them are lawyers of considerable renown. In each House there is a Committee on Judiciary, composed of the strongest and ablest lawyers in each body, which committees give particular study to constitutional questions arising when proposed laws are under consideration.

Because Congress is a coördinate branch, and because of the careful attention the Members of Congress give to constitutional questions arising regarding legislation, it has been held by the United States Supreme Court that no act of Congress should be held to be in violation of the Constitution unless the conflict appears beyond reasonable doubt. Thus the Court said in Ogden *v.* Saunders (12 Wheat. 269): —

> It is but a decent respect due to the wisdom, the integrity, and the patriotism of the legislative body by which any law is passed to presume in favor of its validity until its violation of the Constitution is proved beyond all reasonable doubt.

The Supreme Court has, however, in numerous instances held to be unconstitutional acts of Congress which some of the members of the Supreme Court believed to be entirely in harmony with our fundamental law. In cases such as this there certainly existed a very substantial doubt whether the measure in question was in fact in contravention of the Constitution.

In my opinion, unless a State law or an act of Congress is so clearly unconstitutional that the Court will be unanimous in so declaring, the decision of the Court should uphold the validity of the act.

I think it is generally conceded there is no express authority for the Supreme Court's exercise of power to declare a law unconstitutional. This power has been assumed by the Court as an incident of the exercise of the powers expressly conferred. I believe it is within the power of Congress to prescribe the number of concurring judges necessary in arriving at a decision which shall constitute the decision of the Court. The first section of the bill I have offered requires that where a State law or an act of Congress is declared unconstitutional the court must be unanimous. One dissenting vote will establish the existence of a reasonable doubt. It also provides that the language of an act must be construed literally unless the Court, by unanimous decision, rule otherwise.

Regarding the second section of the bill, I wish merely to say that it is important that every constitutional question be determined at as early a date as possible by the highest court in the land; and, therefore, when any Federal or State law is held unconstitutional by an inferior Federal court, the question should be immediately certified to the United States Supreme Court.

The purpose of this bill is not to allow one, two, three, or four members of the Supreme Court to overrule eight, seven, six, or five members of that distinguished branch of our government; but, rather, to enable one, two, three, or four members of that court to prevent eight, seven, six, or five of its members from overruling the wishes of the nation, as expressed through Congress, or the wishes of a sovereign State, as expressed by its electorate or by its legislature.

I have requested that the bill be printed in the *Record*, and have made this explanation in the hope that the subject will be given discussion by both the laity and the legal fraternity before it comes up for consideration before the Judiciary Committee, to which I ask that it be referred.

APPENDIX E

CHRONOLOGICAL TABLE OF CASES DECIDED BY THE SUPREME COURT OF THE UNITED STATES UNDER THE FOURTEENTH AMENDMENT[1]

October Term, 1872

The Slaughter House Cases	16 Wall. 36
Bradwell *v.* Illinois	16 Wall. 30

October Term, 1873

Bartemeyer *v.* Iowa	18 Wall. 129

October Term, 1874

Minor *v.* Happersett	21 Wall. 162

October Term, 1875

Walker *v.* Sauvinet	92 U. S. 90
Kennard *v.* Louisiana	92 U. S. 480
U. S. *v.* Cruikshank *et al.*	92 U. S. 542
State Railroad Tax Cases (Illinois)	92 U. S. 575

October Term, 1876

Munn *v.* Illinois	94 U. S. 114

October Term, 1877

McMillen *v.* Anderson	95 U. S. 37
Pearson *v.* Yewdall	95 U. S. 294
Davidson *v.* New Orleans	96 U. S. 97
Railroad Co. *v.* Richmond	96 U. S. 521

[1] The more important cases are printed in small capitals.

October Term, 1878

None

October Term, 1879

Strauder *v.* West Virginia	100 U. S. 303
Virginia *v.* Rives	100 U. S. 313
Ex parte Virginia	100 U. S. 339
Kirtland *v.* Hotchkiss	100 U. S. 491
Missouri *v.* Lewis	101 U. S. 22

October Term, 1880

Neal *v.* Delaware	103 U. S. 370

October Term, 1881

Kelly *v.* Pittsburg	104 U. S. 78
Fox *v.* Cincinnati	104 U. S. 783

October Term, 1882

Page *v.* Alabama	106 U. S. 583
U. S. *v.* Harris	106 U. S. 629
Bush *v.* Kentucky	107 U. S. 110
Gross *v.* U. S. Mortgage Co.	108 U. S. 477

October Term, 1883

The Civil Rights Cases	109 U. S. 3
Louisiana *v.* Mayor of New Orleans	109 U. S. 285
Hurtado *v.* California	110 U. S. 516
Santa Cruz Co. *v.* Santa Cruz R. R.	111 U. S. 361
Hagar *v.* Reclamation District 108	111 U. S. 701

October Term, 1884

Head *v.* Amoskeag Mfg. Co.	113 U. S. 9
Barbier *v.* Connolly	113 U. S. 27
Provident Institution *v.* Jersey City	113 U. S. 506
Soon Hing *v.* Crowley	113 U. S. 703
Wurts *v.* Hoagland	114 U. S. 607

October Term, 1885

Kentucky Railroad Tax Cases	115 U. S. 321
Mo. Pac. Ry. Co. *v.* Humes	115 U. S. 512
Campbell *v.* Holt	115 U. S. 620
Presser *v.* Illinois	116 U. S. 252
Sou. Pac. R. R. *v.* California	118 U. S. 109
Arrowsmith *v.* Harmoning	118 U. S. 194
Yick Wo *v.* Hopkins	118 U. S. 356

October Term, 1886

Philadelphia Fire Ins. Co. *v.* New York	119 U. S. 110
Schmidt *v.* Cobb	119 U. S. 286
Hayes *v.* Missouri	120 U. S. 68
Church *v.* Kelsey	121 U. S. 282

October Term, 1887

Spies *v.* Illinois	123 U. S. 131
Sands *v.* Manister River Impr. Co.	123 U. S. 288
Mugler *v.* Kansas	123 U. S. 623
Brooks *v.* Missouri	124 U. S. 394
Pembina Mining Co. *v.* Pennsylvania	125 U. S. 181
Spencer *v.* Merchant	125 U. S. 345
Dow *v.* Beidleman	125 U. S. 680
Robards *v.* Lamb	127 U. S. 58
Mo. Pac. Ry. Co. *v.* Mackey	127 U. S. 205
Minn. & St. L. Ry. Co. *v.* Herrick	127 U. S. 210
Powell *v.* Pennsylvania	127 U. S. 678
Mahon *v.* Justice	127 U. S. 700

October Term, 1888

Kidd *v.* Pearson	128 U. S. 1
Nashville, etc., Ry. *v.* Alabama	128 U. S. 96
Watson *v.* Nevin	128 U. S. 578
Minn. & St. L. Ry. Co. *v.* Beckwith	129 U. S. 26
Baldwin *v.* Kansas	129 U. S. 52
Dent *v.* West Virginia	129 U. S. 114

Marrow *v.* Brinkley	129 U. S. 178
Freeland *v.* Williams	131 U. S. 405

OCTOBER TERM, 1889

Cross *v.* North Carolina	132 U. S. 131
Sugg *v.* Thornton	132 U. S. 524
Palmer *v.* McMahon	133 U. S. 660
Eilenbecker *v.* Plymouth Co.	134 U. S. 31
Bell's Gap R. R. Co. *v.* Pennsylvania	134 U. S. 232
CHICAGO, MIL. & ST. P. RY. *v.* MINNESOTA	134 U. S. 418
Home Ins. Co. *v.* New York	134 U. S. 594
L. & N. R. R. Co. *v.* Woodson	134 U. S. 614
Beatty *v.* Benton	135 U. S. 244
In re Kemmler	136 U. S. 436

OCTOBER TERM, 1890

York *v.* Texas	137 U. S. 15
Crowley *v.* Christensen	137 U. S. 86
Wheeler *v.* Jackson	137 U. S. 245
In re Converse	137 U. S. 624
Caldwell *v.* Texas	137 U. S. 692
Kauffman *v.* Wooters	138 U. S. 285
In re Duncan	139 U. S. 449
Leeper *v.* Texas	139 U. S. 462
In re Manning	139 U. S. 504
Natal *v.* Louisiana	139 U. S. 621
Davis *v.* Texas	139 U. S. 651
Lent *v.* Tillson	140 U. S. 316
Essex Public Road Board *v.* Sprinkle	140 U. S. 334

OCTOBER TERM, 1891

Singer Mfg. Co. *v.* Wright	141 U. S. 696
New Orleans *v.* New Orleans Water Co.	142 U. S. 79
Kaukauna Co. *v.* Canal Co.	142 U. S. 254
Pacific Exp. Co. *v.* Seibert	142 U. S. 339
Charlotte R. R. Co. *v.* Gibbs	142 U. S. 386

Horn Silver Mining Co. *v.* New York	143 U. S. 305
Schwab *v.* Berggren	143 U. S. 442
Felder *v.* Illinois	143 U. S. 452
Budd *v.* New York	143 U. S. 517
Brown *v.* Massachusetts	144 U. S. 573
New York *ex rel.* *v.* Squire	144 U. S. 175
Brown *v.* Smart	144 U. S. 454

OCTOBER TERM, 1892

McPherson *v.* Blacker	146 U. S. 1
Morley *v.* Lake Shore & Mich. S. R. R.	146 U. S. 162
Hallinger *v.* Davis	146 U. S. 314
Yessler *v.* Harbor Commissioners	146 U. S. 646
Thorington *v.* Montgomery	147 U. S. 490
Giozza *v.* Tiernan	148 U. S. 657
Paulsen *v.* Portland	149 U. S. 30
In re Frederich, Petitioner	149 U. S. 70
Minn. & St. L. Ry. Co. *v.* Emmons	149 U. S. 364
McNulty *v.* California	149 U. S. 645

OCTOBER TERM, 1893

Powell *v.* Brunswick Co.	150 U. S. 433
Balt. Trac. Co. *v.* Balt. Belt R. R.	151 U. S. 137
Columbus Sou. Ry. Co. *v.* Wright	151 U. S. 470
N. Y. & N. E. R. R. *v.* Bristol	151 U. S. 556
Lawton *v.* Steele	152 U. S. 133
Montana Co. *v.* St. Louis Mining Co.	152 U. S. 160
Duncan *v.* Missouri	153 U. S. 377
Marchant *v.* Penn. R. R. Co.	153 U. S. 380
Brass *v.* North Dakota	153 U. S. 391
Ashley *v.* Ryan	153 U. S. 436
Miller *v.* Texas	153 U. S. 535
Scott *v.* McNeal	154 U. S. 34
In re Lockwood	154 U. S. 116
REAGAN *v.* FARMERS' LOAN & TRUST CO.	154 U. S. 362
Pittsburg Ry. Co. *v.* Indiana	154 U. S. 421

October Term, 1894

Plumley *v.* Massachusetts	155 U. S. 461
Hooper *v.* California	155 U. S. 648
Andrews *v.* Swarz	156 U. S. 272
Pittsburg Coal Co. *v.* Louisiana	156 U. S. 590
St. L. & San F. Ry. *v.* Gill	156 U. S. 649
Chicago Kan. & W. R. R. *v.* Pontius	157 U. S. 209
Bergeman *v.* Backer	157 U. S. 655
Gray *v.* Conn.	159 U. S. 74
Central Land Co. *v.* Laidley	159 U. S. 103

October Term, 1895

Sweet *v.* Rechel	159 U. S. 380
Winona Land Co. *v.* Minnesota	159 U. S. 526
Moore *v.* Missouri	159 U. S. 673
Kohl *v.* Lehlback	160 U. S. 293
Iowa Cent. Ry. *v.* Iowa	160 U. S. 389
Eldridge *v.* Trezevant	160 U. S. 452
Pearsal *v.* Great Northern Ry.	161 U. S. 646
Gibson *v.* Mississippi	162 U. S. 565
Charley Smith *v.* Mississippi	162 U. S. 592
West. Union Tel. Co. *v.* Taggart	163 U. S. 1
Dibble *v.* Bellingham Bay Land Co.	163 U. S. 63
Lowe *v.* Kansas	163 U. S. 81
Murray *v.* Louisiana	163 U. S. 101
PLESSY *v.* FERGUSON	163 U. S. 537

October Term, 1896

FALLBROOK IRRIGATION CO. *v.* BRADLEY	164 U. S. 112
Tregea *v.* Modesto Irrigation District	164 U. S. 179
MO. PAC. RY. CO. *v.* NEBRASKA	164 U. S. 403
Covington Turnpike Co. *v.* Sandford	164 U. S. 578
St. L. & San F. Ry. Co. *v.* Matthews	165 U. S. 1
Mo. Pac. Ry. Co. *v.* Simmons	165 U. S. 27
GULF, COLO. & SANTA FE RY. *v.* ELLIS	165 U. S. 150
Clarke *v.* McDade	165 U. S. 168

Jones *v.* Brim	165 U. S. 180
Adams Express Co. *v.* Ohio State Auditor	165 U. S. 194
Amer. Express Co. *v.* Indiana	165 U. S. 255
Pim *v.* St. Louis	165 U. S. 273
West. Union Tel. Co. *v.* Indiana	165 U. S. 304
Allgeyer *v.* Louisiana	165 U. S. 578
Allen *v.* Georgia	166 U. S. 138
C. B. & Q. Ry. Co. *v.* Chicago	166 U. S. 226
Gladson *v.* Minnesota	166 U. S. 427
In re Eckart	166 U. S. 481
Zadig *v.* Baldwin	166 U. S. 485
Oxley Stave Co. *v.* Butler Co.	166 U. S. 648
Long Is. W. Supply Co. *v.* Brooklyn	166 U. S. 685
Sentell *v.* N. O. & C. R. R.	166 U. S. 698
L. & N. R. R. Co. *v.* Louisville	166 U. S. 709
Davis *v.* Massachusetts	167 U. S. 43
Wabash R. R. Co. *v.* Defiance	167 U. S. 88
Merchants' Bank *v.* Pennsylvania	167 U. S. 461

OCTOBER TERM, 1897

Turner *v.* New York	168 U. S. 90
Craemer *v.* Washington	168 U. S. 124
Miller *v.* Cornwell R. R. Co.	168 U. S. 131
Hodgson *v.* Vermont	168 U. S. 262
Water Power Co. *v.* Water Commissioners	168 U. S. 349
Nobles *v.* Georgia	168 U. S. 398
Castillo *v.* McConnico	168 U. S. 674
HOLDEN *v.* HARDY	169 U. S. 366
Savings Society *v.* Multnomah Co.	169 U. S. 421
SMYTH *v.* AMES	169 U. S. 466
Backus *v.* Union Depot Co.	169 U. S. 557
Wilson *v.* North Carolina	169 U. S. 586
C. B. & Q. Ry. Co. *v.* Nebraska	170 U. S. 57
Kipley *v.* Illinois	170 U. S. 182
Williams *v.* Mississippi	170 U. S. 213
Houston & Texas Cent. Ry. Co. *v.* Texas	170 U. S. 243
Magoun *v.* Ill. Trust & Savings Bank	170 U. S. 283

Williams *v.* Eggleston	170 U. S. 304
Tinsley *v.* Anderson	171 U. S. 101
King *v.* Mullins	171 U. S. 404

OCTOBER TERM, 1898

MEYER *v.* RICHMOND	172 U. S. 82
Blake *v.* McClung	172 U. S. 239
Norwood *v.* Baker	172 U. S. 269
Bellingham Bay Co. *v.* New Whatcom	172 U. S. 314
Clark *v.* Kansas City	172 U. S. 334
Chappel Chem. Co. *v.* Sulphur Mines Co.	172 U. S. 465
Chappel Chem. Co. *v.* Sulphur Mines Co.	172 U. S. 474
Orient Ins. Co. *v.* Daggs	172 U. S. 557
Conn. Mut. Life Ins. Co. *v.* Spratley	172 U. S. 602
McQuade *v.* Trenton	172 U. S. 636
Wilson *v.* Eureka City	173 U. S. 32
Dewey *v.* Des Moines	173 U. S. 193
St. L., I. M. & St. P. Ry. *v.* Paul	173 U. S. 404
Remington Paper Co. *v.* Watson	173 U. S. 443
Henderson Bridge Co. *v.* Henderson City	173 U. S. 592
Citizens' Nat. Bank *v.* Owensboro	173 U. S. 636
Deposit Bank *v.* Owensboro	173 U. S. 662
Farmers' & Traders' Bank *v.* Owensboro	173 U. S. 663
LAKE SHORE & MICH. S. RY. *v.* SMITH	173 U. S. 684
AM. REFRIG. TRANSIT CO. *v.* HALL	174 U. S. 70
White *v.* Leovy	174 U. S. 91
ATCHISON, TOP. & SANTA FE R. R. *v.* MATTHEWS	174 U. S. 96
Kentucky Tax Cases (six)	174 U. S. 408
San Diego Land Co. *v.* National City	174 U. S. 739
Cal. Nat. Bank *v.* Thomas	171 U. S. 441
New York State *v.* Roberts	171 U. S. 658

OCTOBER TERM, 1899

Scudder *v.* Comptr. of New York	175 U. S. 32
Brown *v.* New Jersey	175 U. S. 172
Markuson *v.* Boucher	175 U. S. 184

Ark. Bldg. Assn. *v.* Madden	175 U. S. 269
Tullis *v.* Lake Erie & Western R. R.	175 U. S. 348
Abbott *v.* Tacoma Bank	175 U. S. 409
CUMMINGS *v.* BOARD OF EDUCATION	175 U. S. 528
Keokuk & Hamilton Bridge Co. *v.* Illinois	175 U. S. 626
Bolln *v.* Nebraska	176 U. S. 83
Clark *v.* Kansas City	176 U. S. 114
Chicago, Mil. & St. P. Ry *v.* Tompkins	176 U. S. 167
Adirondack Ry. *v.* New York State	176 U. S. 335
Roller *v.* Holly	176 U. S. 398
Weyerhaneser *v.* Minnesota	176 U. S. 550
MAXWELL *v.* DOW	176 U. S. 581
Waters Pierce Oil Co. *v.* Texas	177 U. S. 28
Petit *v.* Minnesota	177 U. S. 165
Henkel *v.* Cincinnati	177 U. S. 171
Gundling *v.* Chicago	177 U. S. 183
Ohio Oil Co. *v.* Indiana	177 U. S. 190
L. & N. R. R. Co. *v.* Schmidt	177 U. S. 230
Saranac Land Co. *v.* Comptr. of New York	177 U. S. 318
Minn. & St. L. Ry. Co. *v.* Gardner	177 U. S. 332
CARTER *v.* TEXAS	177 U. S. 442
Erb *v.* Morasch	177 U. S. 584
L'Hote *v.* New Orleans	177 U. S. 587
Osborne *v.* San Diego Co.	178 U. S. 22
Sully *v.* Am. Nat. Bank	178 U. S. 289
Wheeler *v.* N. Y., N. H. & H. R. R.	178 U. S. 321
N. Y. Life Ins. Co. *v.* Cravens	178 U. S. 389
TAYLOR & MARSHALL *v.* BECKHAM	178 U. S. 548

OCTOBER TERM, 1900

Looker *v.* Maynard	179 U. S. 46
Am. Sugar Ref. Co. *v.* Louisiana	179 U. S. 89
Chapin *v.* Fye	179 U. S. 127
William *v.* Fears	179 U. S. 270
New York State *v.* Barker	179 U. S. 279
Wis., Minn. & Pac. R. R. *v.* Jacobson	179 U. S. 287
Mason *v.* Missouri	179 U. S. 328

Austin *v.* Tennessee	179 U. S. 343
Davis *v.* Burke	179 U. S. 399
Tyler *v.* Judge of Court of Registration	179 U. S. 405
Loeb *v.* Columbia Township Trustees	179 U. S. 472
Gusman *v.* Marrers	180 U. S. 81
Lamposas *v.* Bell	180 U. S. 276
N. O. Debenture Co. *v.* Louisiana	180 U. S. 320
W. W. Cargill Co. *v.* Minnesota	180 U. S. 452
Minn. *v.* Brundage	180 U. S. 499
Freeport W. Co. *v.* Freeport City	180 U. S. 587
Lombard *v.* W. Chicago Park Commissioners	181 U. S. 33
Eastern Bldg. Assn. *v.* Welling	181 U. S. 47
Hancock Mut. Life Ins. Co. *v.* Warren	181 U. S. 73
Am. Sugar Ref. Co. *v.* New Orleans	181 U. S. 277
French *v.* Barber Asphalt Paving Co.	181 U. S. 324
Tonawanda *v.* Lyon	181 U. S. 389
Webster *v.* Fargo	181 U. S. 394
Cass Farm Co. *v.* Detroit	181 U. S. 396
Detroit *v.* Parker	181 U. S. 399
Shumate *v.* Heman	181 U. S. 402
Farrel *v.* W. Chicago Park Commissioners	181 U. S. 404
Red River Valley Bank *v.* Craig	181 U. S. 548
Mallett *v.* North Carolina	181 U. S. 589
Carson *v.* Sewer Commissioners	182 U. S. 398
Simon *v.* Craft	182 U. S. 427

October Term, 1901

Cotting *v.* Kansas City Stock Yds. Co.	183 U. S. 79
Storti *v.* Massachusetts	183 U. S. 138
Capital City Dairy Co. *v.* Ohio	183 U. S. 238
Orr *v.* Gillman	183 U. S. 278
Gallup *v.* Schmidt	183 U. S. 300
Florida Central & Penin. R. R. *v.* Reynolds	183 U. S. 471
L. & N. R. R. Co. *v.* Kentucky	183 U. S. 503
Nutting *v.* Massachusetts	183 U. S. 553
Minder *v.* Georgia	183 U. S. 559
Chicago, R. I. & Pac. R. R. *v.* Zernecke	183 U. S. 582

King *v.* Portland City	184 U. S. 61
Voight *v.* Detroit City	184 U. S. 115
League *v.* Texas	184 U. S. 156
Clark *v.* Titusville	184 U. S. 329
Rothschild *v.* Knight	184 U. S. 334
Skaneateles W. W. Co. *v.* Skaneateles	184 U. S. 354
Booth *v.* Illinois	184 U. S. 426
Goodrich *v.* Detroit	184 U. S. 432
CONNOLLY *v.* UNION SEWER PIPE CO.	184 U. S. 540
Erie R. R. Co. *v.* Purdy	185 U. S. 148
St. L. Coal Co. *v.* Illinois	185 U. S. 203
Fid. Mut. Life Assn. *v.* Mettler	185 U. S. 308
N. O. W. W. Co. *v.* Louisiana	185 U. S. 336
Trav. Ins. Co. *v.* Connecticut	185 U. S. 364
Minn. & St. L. R. R. Co. *v.* Minnesota	186 U. S. 257

OCTOBER TERM, 1902

Turpin *v.* Lemon	187 U. S. 51
Dreyer *v.* Illinois	187 U. S. 71
Jacobi *v.* Alabama	187 U. S. 133
Home for Incurables *v.* City of New York	187 U. S. 155
Layton *v.* Missouri	187 U. S. 356
Chadwick *v.* Kelly	187 U. S. 540
Manley *v.* Park	187 U. S. 547
Tellmidge Power Co. *v.* Rio Grande Ry.	187 U. S. 569
Otis *v.* Parker	187 U. S. 606
Billings *v.* Illinois	188 U. S. 97
Blackstone *v.* Miller	188 U. S. 189
Hooker *v.* Los Angeles	188 U. S. 314
Louisville, etc., Ferry Co. *v.* Kentucky	188 U. S. 385
Williams *v.* Parker	188 U. S. 491
Reetz *v.* Michigan	188 U. S. 505
Tarrance *v.* Florida	188 U. S. 519
PROUT *v.* STARR	188 U. S. 537
Kidd *v.* Alabama	188 U. S. 730
Sawyer *v.* Piper	189 U. S. 154
Davis Mfg. Co. *v.* Los Angeles	189 U. S. 207

Glidden *v.* Harrington	189 U. S. 255
Farmers' Ins. Co. *v.* Dabney	189 U. S. 301
Detroit Ry. *v.* Osborn	189 U. S. 383
Brownfield *v.* South Carolina	189 U. S. 426
Knoxville W. Co. *v.* Knoxville	189 U. S. 434
San Diego Land Co. *v.* Jasper	189 U. S. 439
Giles *v.* Harris	189 U. S. 475
West. Union Tel. Co. *v.* Gottlieb	190 U. S. 412

October Term, 1903

Howard *v.* Fleming	191 U. S. 126
Smith *v.* Indiana	191 U. S. 138
Missouri *v.* Dockery	191 U. S. 165
Atkin *v.* Kansas	191 U. S. 207
Hibben *v.* Smith	191 U. S. 310
Board of Assessors *v.* Comptoir National	191 U. S. 388
Arbuckle *v.* Blackburn	191 U. S. 405
Wabash R. R. Co. *v.* Flannigan	192 U. S. 29
Postal Tel. Cab. Co. *v.* New Hope	192 U. S. 55
Cronin *v.* Adams	192 U. S. 108
Stanislaus Co. *v.* San Joaquin C. I. & Co.	192 U. S. 201
Rogers *v.* Alabama	192 U. S. 226
Butfield *v.* Stranahan	192 U. S. 470
Adams *v.* New York	192 U. S. 585
Cinn. St. Ry. Co. *v.* Snell	193 U. S. 30
Minn. & St. L. R. R. *v.* Minnesota	193 U. S. 53
Leigh *v.* Green	193 U. S. 79
Giles *v.* Teasley	193 U. S. 146
Barney *v.* City of New York	193 U. S. 430
Rippey *v.* Texas	193 U. S. 504
Gr. Sou. Hotel Co. *v.* Jones	193 U. S. 532
Newburyport W. Co. *v.* Newburyport	193 U. S. 561
Pope *v.* Williams	193 U. S. 621
West *v.* Louisiana	194 U. S. 258
M. K. & T. Ry. Co. *v.* May	194 U. S. 267
Fischer *v.* St. Louis	194 U. S. 361
Lloyd *v.* Dollison	194 U. S. 445

Shepard *v.* Barron	194 U. S. 553
T. H. & Ind. R. R. *v.* Indiana	194 U. S. 579
Field *v.* Barber Asphalt Co.	194 U. S. 618
Bradley *v.* Lightcap	195 U. S. 1

October Term, 1904

Aikens *v.* Wisconsin	195 U. S. 194
Dobbins *v.* Los Angeles	195 U. S. 223
Nat. Exchange Bank *v.* Wiley	195 U. S. 257
Olsen *v.* Smith	195 U. S. 332
Seattle *v.* Kelleher	195 U. S. 351
Helena W. W. Co. *v.* Helena	195 U. S. 383
Harding *v.* Illinois	196 U. S. 78
Madisonville Trac. Co. *v.* Mining Co.	196 U. S. 239
Cook *v.* Marshall Co.	196 U. S. 261
Hodge *v.* Muscatine Co.	196 U. S. 276
Smiley *v.* Kansas	196 U. S. 447
Corry *v.* Baltimore	196 U. S. 466
Coulter *v.* L. & N. R. R. Co.	196 U. S. 599
Scottish Union Ins. Co. *v.* Bowland	196 U. S. 611
Jacobson *v.* Massachusetts	197 U. S. 11
Kehrer *v.* Stewart	197 U. S. 60
Nat. Cotton Oil Co. *v.* Texas	197 U. S. 115
Sou. Cotton Oil Co. *v.* Texas	197 U. S. 134
Dallemagne *v.* Moisan	197 U. S. 169
Dawson *v.* Columbia Trust Co.	197 U. S. 178
L. & N. R. R. Co. *v.* Barber Asphalt Co.	197 U. S.430
N. O. Gas Co. *v.* Drainage Commission	197 U. S. 453
Iron Cliffs Co. *v.* Negaunee Iron Co.	197 U. S. 463
Muhlker *v.* New York & Harlem R. R. Co.	197 U. S. 544
Lochner *v.* New York	198 U. S. 45
Empire State Mining Co. *v.* Hanley	198 U. S. 292
Del., L. & W. R. R. *v.* Pennsylvania	198 U. S. 341
Clark *v.* Nash	198 U. S. 361
Birrel *v.* New York & Harlem R. R. Co.	198 U. S. 390
S. T. & I. H. Ry. Co. *v.* Savannah	198 U. S. 392
Cunius *v.* Reading School Dist.	198 U. S. 458

Ah Sin *v.* Wittman	198 U. S. 501
Met. St. Ry. *v.* New York	199 U. S. 1
Farrell *v.* O'Brien	199 U. S. 89

October Term, 1905

Union Transit Co. *v.* Kentucky	199 U. S. 194
Marvin *v.* Trou	199 U. S. 212
Kies *v.* Lowrey	199 U. S. 233
French *v.* Taylor	199 U. S. 274
Reduction Co. *v.* Sanitary Works	199 U. S. 306
Gardner *v.* Michigan	199 U. S. 325
Jack *v.* Kansas	199 U. S. 372
Carrol *v.* Greenwich Ins. Co.	199 U. S. 401
Rogers *v.* Peck	199 U. S. 425
Manigault *v.* Springs	199 U. S. 473
Lieberman *v.* Van de Carr	199 U. S. 552
Minn. Iron Co. *v.* Kline	199 U. S. 593
Water Co. *v.* Knoxville	200 U. S. 22
Waterworks Co. *v.* Owensboro	200 U. S. 38
Gas Co. *v.* Peoria	200 U. S. 49
Campbell *v.* California	200 U. S. 87
Mead *v.* Portland	200 U. S. 148
Howard *v.* Kentucky	200 U. S. 164
Armour Packing Co. *v.* Lacy	200 U. S. 226
Carfer *v.* Caldwell	200 U. S. 293
Martin *v.* Texas	200 U. S. 316
Strickley *v.* Highland Mining Co.	200 U. S. 527
C. B. & Q. Ry. *v.* Drainage Commission	200 U. S. 561
Kentucky *v.* Powers	201 U. S. 1
Felts *v.* Murphy	201 U. S. 123
Valentina *v.* Mercer	201 U. S. 131
Otis Co. *v.* Ludlow Co.	201 U. S. 140
Mich. Cent. R. R. *v.* Powers	201 U. S. 245
Keen *v.* Keen	201 U. S. 319
Soper *v.* Lawrence Bros.	201 U. S. 359
W. Chicago R. R. *v.* Chicago	201 U. S. 506
St. John *v.* New York	201 U. S. 633

Rawlins *v.* Georgia	201 U. S. 638
SECURITY MUT. LIFE INS. CO. *v.* PREWITT	202 U. S. 246
Hulbert *v.* Chicago.	202 U. S. 275
Devine *v.* Los Angeles	202 U. S. 313
Cox *v.* Texas	202 U. S. 446
N. Y. Cent. R. R. *v.* Miller	202 U. S. 584

OCTOBER TERM, 1906

HODGES *v.* U. S.	203 U. S. 1
Nat. Coun. U. A. M. *v.* State Coun. U. A. M.	203 U. S. 151
Petroleum Co. *v.* West Virginia	203 U. S. 183
Nat. Life Ins. Co. *v.* Riggs	203 U. S. 243
A. C. L. R. R. Co. *v.* Ellis	203 U. S. 256
S. A. L. Ry. *v.* Florida	203 U. S. 261
Martin *v.* P. & L. E. R. R. Co.	203 U. S. 284
Security Trust Co. *v.* City of Lexington	203 U. S. 323
Offield *v.* N. Y., N. H. & H. R. R. Co.	203 U. S. 372
Fairhaven & W. R. R. Co. *v.* New Haven	203 U. S. 379
A. & V. Ry. Co. *v.* Miss. R. R. Commission	203 U. S. 496
Gatewood *v.* North Carolina	203 U. S. 531
Cahen *v.* Brewster	203 U. S. 543
Board of Education *v.* Illinois	203 U. S. 553
Old Wayne Life Assn. *v.* McDonough	204 U. S. 8
Bachtel *v.* Wilson	204 U. S. 36
Cleveland Elec. Ry. *v.* Cleveland	204 U. S. 116
Hatch *v.* Reardon	204 U. S. 152
Ballard *v.* Hunter	204 U. S. 241
Bacon *v.* Walker	204 U. S. 311
West. Turf Assn. *v.* Greenberg	204 U. S. 359
C. B. & Q. Ry. *v.* Babcock	204 U. S. 585
Coffey *v.* County of Harlan	204 U. S. 659
Halter *v.* Nebraska	205 U. S. 34
W. Star Mfg. Co. *v.* Fulton	205 U. S. 60
Tracy *v.* Ginsburg	205 U. S. 170
Urquart *v.* Brown	205 U. S. 179
Mining Co. *v.* Hanley	205 U. S. 225
Met. Life Ins. Co. *v.* New Orleans	205 U. S. 395

Patterson *v.* Colorado	205 U. S. 454
Chanler *v.* Kelsey	205 U. S. 466
Barrington *v.* Missouri	205 U. S. 483
A. C. L. R. R. Co. *v.* North Carolina Corp. Com.	206 U. S. 1
BUCK *v.* BEACH	206 U. S. 392
Sauer *v.* City of New York	206 U. S. 536
OCTOBER TERM, 1907	
RAYMOND, TREAS. *v.* CHICAGO TRAC. CO.	207 U. S. 20
Lee *v.* New Jersey	207 U. S. 65
S. A. L. Ry. *v.* Seegars	207 U. S. 73
Interstate Ry. Co. *v.* Massachusetts	207 U. S. 79
Leathe *v.* Thomas	207 U. S. 93
CENT. OF GA. RY. CO. *v.* WRIGHT	207 U. S. 127
Chambers *v.* B. & O. R. R. Co.	207 U. S. 142
Hunter *v.* Pittsburg	207 U. S. 161
Schoener *v.* Pennsylvania	207 U. S. 188
Ozan L. Co. *v.* Union Co. Bank	207 U. S. 251
Polk *v.* Mutual Reserve Fund	207 U. S. 310
Heath & M. Co. *v.* Worst	207 U. S. 338
Vandalia R. R. Co. *v.* Indiana	207 U. S. 359
Rendering Co. *v.* Vermont	207 U. S. 541
Cosmopolitan Club *v.* Virginia	208 U. S. 378
Muller *v.* Oregon	208 U. S. 412
Phillips *v.* Mobile	208 U. S. 472
Richard *v.* Mobile	208 U. S. 480
Ughbanks *v.* Armstrong	208 U. S. 481
Disconto Gesellschaft *v.* Umbreit	208 U. S. 570
U. P. Ry. Co. *v.* Duluth	208 U. S. 583
Hairston *v.* D. &. W. Ry. Co.	208 U. S. 598
Ex parte YOUNG	209 U. S. 125
General Oil Co. *v.* Crain	209 U. S. 211
Thomas *v.* Iowa	209 U. S. 258
Thompson *v.* Kentucky	209 U. S. 340
Hudson County W. Co. *v.* McArthur	209 U. S. 349
Longyear *v.* Toolan	209 U. S. 414
Stickney *v.* Kelsey	209 U. S. 419

Lang *v.* New Jersey	209 U. S. 467
Cent. R. R. Co. *v.* New Jersey	209 U. S. 473
C. C. C. & St. L. Ry. Co. *v.* Porter	210 U. S. 177
M. J. & K. C. R. R. Co. *v.* Mississippi	210 U. S. 187
Delmar Jockey Club *v.* Missouri	210 U. S. 324
Londoner *v.* Denver	210 U. S. 373

October Term, 1908

Bailey *v.* Alabama	211 U. S. 452
Twining *v.* New Jersey	211 U. S. 78
Paddell *v.* City of New York	211 U. S. 446
Silz *v.* Hesterberg	211 U. S. 31
Berea College *v.* Kentucky	211 U. S. 45
Home Tel. Co. *v.* Los Angeles	211 U. S. 265
McClean *v.* Arkansas	211 U. S. 539
Cold Storage Co. *v.* Chicago	211 U. S. 306
Lemieux *v.* Young	211 U. S. 489
Beers *v.* Glynn	211 U. S. 477
Rusch *v.* John Duncan Co.	211 U. S. 526
Prentis *v.* A. C. L. R. R. *et al.*	211 U. S. 210
McCorquodale *v.* Texas	211 U. S. 432
Hammond Pack. Co. *v.* Arkansas	212 U. S. 322
Moyer *v.* Peabody	212 U. S. 78
Waters Pierce Oil Co *v.* Texas	212 U. S. 86
Waters Pierce Oil Co. *v.* Texas	212 U. S. 113
L. & N. R. R. Co. *v.* Cent. Stock Yds. Co.	212 U. S. 132
Ontario Land Co. *v.* Yordy	212 U. S. 152
Wilcox *et al.* *v.* Consolidated Gas Co.	212 U. S. 19
Knoxville *v.* Water Co.	212 U. S. 1
Thomas *v.* Texas	212 U. S. 278
Bonner *v.* Gorman	213 U. S. 86
Keerl *v.* Montana	213 U. S. 135
Siler *v.* L. & N. R. R. Co.	213 U. S. 175
Selliger *v.* Kentucky	213 U. S. 200
Boise Water Co. *v.* Boise City	213 U. S. 277
Goodrich *v.* Ferris	214 U. S. 71

Welch *v.* Swasey *et al.*	214 U. S. 91
St. P. M. & M. Ry. Co. *v.* Minnesota	214 U. S. 497
Fid. & Cas. Co. *v.* Sou. Ry. News Co.	214 U. S. 498

October Term, 1909

Scott County Road *v.* Hines	215 U. S. 336
Marbles *v.* Creecy	215 U. S. 63
Bank *v.* City Council	215 U. S. 341
Withnell *v.* Construction Co.	216 U. S. 603
West. Union Tel. Co. *v.* Kansas	216 U. S. 1
Pullman Co. *v.* Kansas	216 U. S. 56
Ludwig *v.* West. U. Tel. Co.	216 U. S. 146
King *v.* West Virginia *et al.*	216 U. S. 92
Sou. Ry. Co. *v.* Greene	216 U. S. 400
Mo. Pac. Ry. Co. *v.* Kansas	216 U. S. 262
Cemetery Co. *v.* San Francisco	216 U. S. 358
N. O. *et al. v.* N. Y. Life Ins. Co.	216 U. S. 517
Lumber Co. *v.* Mississippi	217 U. S. 433
Mo. Pac. Ry. Co. *v.* Nebraska	217 U. S. 196
Boston Chamber of Commerce *v.* Boston	217 U. S. 191
Fay *v.* Crozer	217 U. S. 455
Citizen's Bank *v.* Kentucky	217 U. S. 443
Kidd & Co. *v.* Musselman Gro. Co.	217 U. S. 461
Brown Forman Co. *v.* Kentucky	217 U. S. 563
S. W. Oil Co. *v.* Texas	217 U. S. 114
Standard Oil Co. *v.* Tennessee	217 U. S. 413
Williams *v.* Arkansas	217 U. S. 79
Rhodus *v.* Manning	217 U. S. 597
Vought *v.* Wisconsin	217 U. S. 590
L. & N. R. R. Co. *v.* Melton	218 U. S. 36
Shelvin Carpenter Co. *v.* Minnesota	218 U. S. 57
Franklin *v.* South Carolina	218 U. S. 161
Watson *v.* Maryland	218 U. S. 173

October Term, 1910

Cincinnati I. & W. Ry. *v.* Connorsville	218 U. S. 336
Moffitt *v.* Kelly	218 U. S. 400

West. Union Tel. Co. *v.* Commercial Milling Co.	218 U. S. 409
I. C. R. R. Co. *v.* Kentucky	218 U. S. 551
Griffith *v.* Connecticut	218 U. S. 563
Griffith *v.* Connecticut	218 U. S. 572
Calder *v.* Michigan	218 U. S. 591
Memphis *v.* Cumberland Tel. Co.	218 U. S. 624
Mobile J. & K. C. R. R. *v.* Turnipseed	219 U. S. 35
American Land Co. *v.* Zeiss	219 U. S. 47
Noble State Bank *v.* Haskell	219 U. S. 105
Shallenberger *v.* First State Bank	219 U. S. 114
Assaria State Bank *v.* Dolley	219 U. S. 121
Enzel *v.* O'Malley	219 U. S. 128
Kentucky Union Co. *v.* Kentucky	219 U. S. 140
House *v.* Mayes	219 U. S. 270
Broadnax *v.* Missouri	219 U. S. 285
German Alliance Ins. Co. *v.* Hale	219 U. S. 307
Chicago, R. I. & Pac. R. R. *v.* Arkansas	219 U. S. 453
C. B. & Q. R. R. *v.* McGuire	219 U. S. 549
Noble State Bank *v.* Haskell	219 U. S. 575
Lindsley *v.* Nat. Carbonic Gas Co.	220 U. S. 61
Shawnee Sewerage & Drainage Co. *v.* Stearns	220 U. S. 462
Sperry & Hutchinson Co. *v.* Rhodes	220 U. S. 502
OKLAHOMA *v.* KANSAS NAT. GAS CO.	221 U. S. 229
Liverpool Ins. Co. *v.* Orleans Assessors	221 U. S. 346
Orient Ins. Co. *v.* Orleans Assessors	221 U. S. 358
Fifth Ave. Coach Co. *v.* New York	221 U. S. 467
Appleby *v.* City of Buffalo	221 U. S. 524
Provident Institution *v.* Malone	221 U. S. 660

APPENDIX F

CHART No. VII

SUMMARY CHART OF ALL DECISIONS BY THE U. S. SUPREME COURT UNDER THE FOURTEENTH AMENDMENT

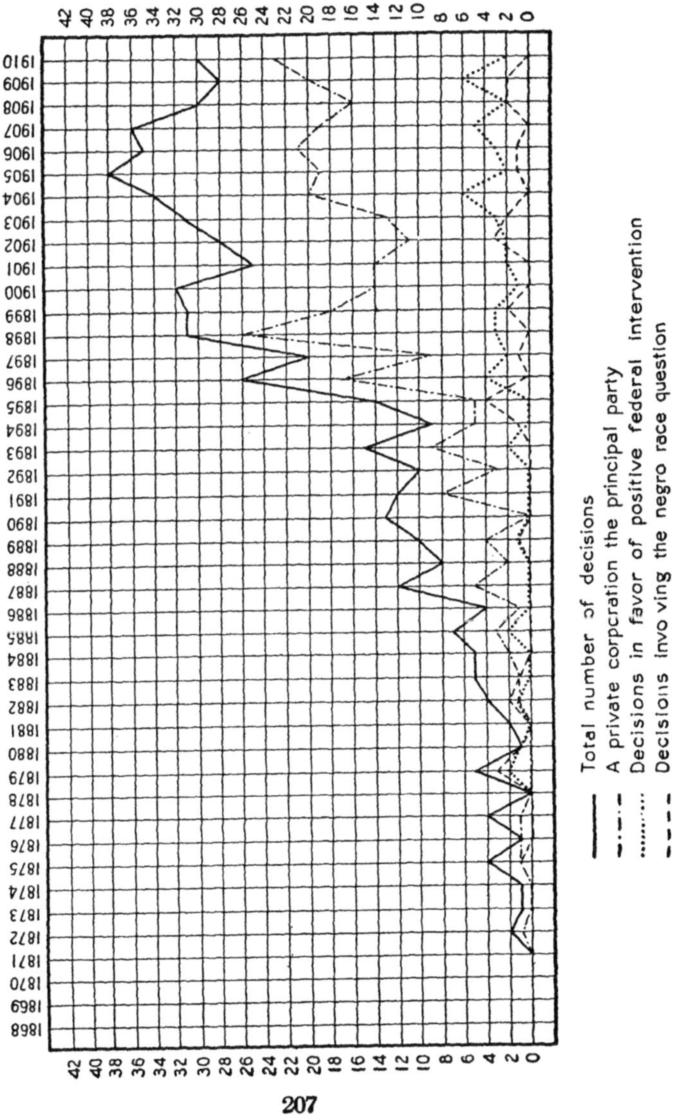

INDEX

INDEX

GPSR Compliance

The European Union's (EU) General Product Safety Regulation (GPSR) is a set of rules that requires consumer products to be safe and our obligations to ensure this.

If you have any concerns about our products, you can contact us on ProductSafety@springernature.com

In case Publisher is established outside the EU, the EU authorized representative is:

Springer Nature Customer Service Center GmbH
Europaplatz 3
69115 Heidelberg, Germany

Batch number: 10844627

Printed by Printforce, the Netherlands